Monetary Control in the United Kingdom

M.J. ARTIS
University of Manchester

&

M.K. LEWIS
University of Adelaide

Philip Allan

First published 1981 by
PHILIP ALLAN PUBLISHERS LIMITED
MARKET PLACE
DEDDINGTON
OXFORD OX5 4SE (UK)

.

British Library Cataloguing in Publication Data
Artis, M. J.
Monetary control in the United Kingdom.
1. Monetary policy — Great Britain
I. Title II. Lewis, M. K.
332.4'941 HG939.5

ISBN 0—86003—040—7
ISBN 0—86003—137—3 Pbk

Set by MHL Typesetting Limited, Coventry
Printed in Great Britain at the Camelot Press Limited, Southampton

Contents

Preface   iv

1. Rethinking Monetary Controls   1
   Policy in the 1960s; Reforms of 1971; Reforms of 1980

2. The Demand for Money   11
   Theoretical considerations; Empirical Studies Before 1971;
   Research Since 1971; Stability of Demand for Money;
   Short Run Control

3. Monetary Targets   38
   Role of Monetary Targets; Effects of Monetary Policy;
   Transmission Mechanisms; Exchange Rate Considerations;
   DCE versus Money; Narrow Money; Which Broad Money
   Aggregate?

4. Controlling the Supply of Money   61
   Controls Over Interest Rates; Factors Affecting the Money
   Supply; External Influences; PSBR and Gilt Sales; Bank
   Lending

5. Bank Intermediation   86
   Retail Banking; Wholesale Banking; Prudential Regulation

6. Methods of Monetary Control   108
   Direct Controls; Bank and Non-Bank Responses to Interest
   Rates; Monetary Base Control

7. Some Problems of the 1980s   132
   Bank Lending, Fiscal Policy and Monetary Control; Exchange
   Controls and Monetary Policy; Membership of EMS and
   Exchange Rate Policies

Bibliography   146

Index   153

Preface

This book provides an up-to-date guide to the aims of monetary policy in Britain and the methods of monetary control. At the time of writing (April 1981), the latter are undergoing alteration. We explain the factors which have led to this revision and ask whether the new and proposed procedures constitute a viable system of control. A major theme developed is that simple views like 'control the money supply via interest rates' or 'control the money supply via the monetary base' will not do in a financial system as sophisticated as Britain's. An environment in which financial institutions compete vigorously for deposits and loans in a variety of currencies for a variety of maturities, producing intermediary services in a variety of markets in a variety of ways, puts any system of controls to the test. Such conditions can lead, in the longer run, to a state of affairs in which the money supply may be unable to be either controlled or defined satisfactorily.

The genesis of the book owes much to the time one of us (Mervyn Lewis) spent in 1979–1980 as Visiting Scholar, Economics Division, Bank of England. He wishes to thank Charles Goodhart and others for making this possible. The intellectual indebtedness to Dr. Goodhart will be apparent. Others at the Bank whose views find reflection here, although they cannot be specifically acknowledged, are Michael Foot, Tony Hotson, Andrew Threadgold and Chris Davies. Kevin Davis of the University of Adelaide kindly read the whole draft and made valuable comments. Also at Adelaide, Helen Wickens and Kath Cheshire provided valuable research assistance, and Kerry Clift cheerfully and speedily typed the whole manuscript. Otton Solis, at Manchester University, provided the book with an index.

M. J. Artis, University of Manchester
M. K. Lewis, University of Adelaide

1

Rethinking Monetary Controls

Monetary policy is continually adapting to events as new problems arise which require new solutions. It is also influenced by (and influences) the evolution of the financial system. But the changes introduced in 1979 and 1980 signal something more — a deliberate effort by the authorities to rethink the basis of monetary controls. Exchange controls were abolished in October 1979; in the same month a new Banking Act came into force to determine which institutions could continue to operate as banks. Enactment of this legislation provided an opportunity to review the arrangements for banks' (and now other deposit-taking institutions') capital adequacy, foreign exchange exposure (where appropriate), and liquidity.[1] An extensive review of the methods of monetary control was undertaken by the Bank of England and the Treasury, and in March 1980 a consultation paper was published (hereafter referred to as the Green Paper).[2] Discussion ensued amongst the authorities, bankers, journalists and academics. From this has resulted the abolition of the supplementary special deposits scheme familiarly known as the 'corset' (in June 1980), an announcement of the ending of the reserve asset ratio (announced in November 1980) and its interim reduction from 12.5 to 10% (in January 1981), new operational techniques for open market operations (which began in November 1980), alterations to the cash reserve requirement (announced in March 1981), and experimentation with systems of monetary base control (foreshadowed in March 1981). This book seeks to explain the reasoning behind these changes, to take stock of where they are leading, and assess the adequacy of monetary controls in the new environment.

Our starting point is to note that a ten yearly cycle in monetary reform has been confirmed by recent changes, for each of the three previous decades in Britain has begun with revisions to the system of monetary controls. In 1951 a Conservative Government, aiming to break away from rationing and direct controls, 'rediscovered' Bank rate as a technique of credit control (although it soon rediscovered controls over lending of the clearing banks). At the beginning of the 1960s the first calls were made to the new Special Deposits scheme, so strengthening direct controls, but the base of policy was broadened by the extension of lending directives (or advances requests) to non-clearing banks and finance houses. Both of these themes — the mixture of direct controls *vis-à-vis* interest rates, and the area of monetary control — were again in evidence in the reforms of 1971. Competition and Credit Control signalled a second rediscovery of interest rates, as a means of reducing reliance upon direct controls and making for competition in the financial sector, combined with an extension of the remaining controls to all banks and finance houses. These same themes once again feature in the most recent revisions. Indeed, it is our contention that the '1980 reforms' should be seen as a continuation of the original aims of Competition and Credit Control.

Policy in the 1960s

The aims of Competition and Credit Control were a direct response to the distortions which resulted from the pre-existing techniques of monetary policy, but indicated also a belief that a non-discriminatory system of controls could be found. Despite the (first) rediscovery of interest rates and the extension of moral suasion to all banks, the London clearing banks had been singled out for the application of portfolio controls and interest rate regulations. In the company of the Scottish banks alone, they were subject to the Special Deposits scheme, whereby funds could be called to, and frozen in, special accounts at the Bank of England to reinforce, and in some cases substitute for, advances requests. London clearing banks were required to maintain both a 'primary' cash reserve ratio (of currency and Bank of England balances to deposits) and a 'secondary' liquid assets ratio (where liquid assets included cash, money at call and bills). Only these banks and their counterparts in Scotland and Northern Ireland adhered to interest rate ceilings upon deposit and loan rates, which were linked by custom to the Bank of England's Bank rate determination.

Sustained reliance upon these controls meant that the clearing banks bore the brunt of policy changes. Figure 1.1 shows the incurrence of liabilities to non-bank residents of the UK by four major groups of financial institutions:

(i)   deposit banks (London and Scottish clearing banks, Northern Ireland banks and the smaller cheque paying banks);
(ii) other banks (accepting houses, discount houses, foreign banks and other UK banks);
(iii) insurance offices and pension funds;
(iv) other non-bank institutions (building societies, finance houses, trusts and savings banks).

The data are annual from 1952 to 1969, calculated from flow of funds and deposit classifications of the Bank of England. Based upon Bank rate movements and policy statements, periods of restrictive policy can be identified in 1955, 1957–8, 1964, 1966 and 1969. Each instance is marked by a sharp curtailment of deposit banks' liabilities. To judge from changes in liabilities, the 'unregulated' institutions were by no means immune to the operation of policy. However, their response was less and lagged relative to that of the deposit banks.

As well as suffering the differential impact of monetary policy during periods of restriction, the secular growth of the clearing banks was also affected. Table 1.1 gives details of the total balance sheets of British financial institutions for various dates from 1960 to 1979 and the compound annual rates of growth over various intervals of time. The clearing banks declined in size relative to other institutions during the

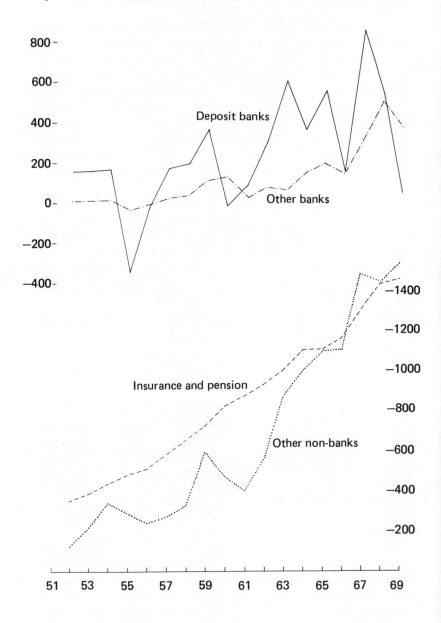

Figure 1.1 *Incurrence of Liabilities by Major Financial Groups 1952–69 (£m)*

Table 1.1 Liabilities of Financial Institutions

	Amount (£ million)					Compound Annual Rates of Growth			
	1960	1965	1970	1975	1979	1960–5	1965–70	1970–5	1975–9
Major Deposit Banks									
Resident	8,618	10,760	12,234	26,223	43,964	4.54	2.60	16.47	13.80
Non-Resident				3,814	8,193				21.06
Discount Houses	1,197	1,455	2,352	2,536	4,568	3.98	10.08	1.52	15.85
Accepting Houses									
Resident*	(134)†	530	1,287	2,356	3,920	31.65	19.42	12.85	13.57
Non-Resident	250	398	1,238	1,865	3,713	9.75	25.48	8.54	18.78
Other Banks									
Resident*	(286)†	1,012	4,527	16,293	29,357	30.44	34.94	29.19	15.85
Non-Resident	1,096	3,000	15,042	60,858	123,001	22.31	38.05	32.25	19.23
National Savings Banks	1,710	1,822	1,752	2,141	3,363	1.28	−0.78	4.09	11.95
Trustee Savings Banks	1,328	2,017	2,481	3,668	5,805	8.72	4.22	8.13	12.16
Finance Houses	678	1,108	1,222	1,199/1,512	3,470	10.32	1.98	−0.38	23.08
Building Societies	3,183	5,577	10,940	24,364	46,126	11.87	14.43	17.37	17.30
Investment and Unit Trusts	2,166	3,699	5,949	8,651	10,759	11.29	9.97	7.77	5.60
Insurance Offices	6,344	9,866	15,452	27,891	52,797	9.23	9.39	12.54	17.30
Pension Funds	3,309	5,385	7,765	13,680	34,148	10.23	7.59	11.99	25.70

* Excludes UK banks' holdings of Non-Sterling Currency Deposits   †Estimated

1960s. By contrast the accepting houses and other non-clearing banks, largely free of controls, expanded their business (resident and non-resident) at a very fast rate. Insofar as policy relied upon restraining intermediation by the clearing banks, it was operating upon a steadily contracting base. Considerations of equity alone called for some evening up of competition as between the different classes of bank. Add this to the growing irksomeness of operating the system of controls, and the incentives for the authorities to want to alter both competitive practices and the techniques of credit control are clear.

It was against this backdrop that studies of the demand for money function, relating the public's holdings of money to income and interest rates, assumed importance in providing intellectual support for a break from direct controls. A reasonably stable demand for money function is the foundation stone of the link between the quantity of money on the one hand, and income and prices on the other. Empirical studies undertaken at the Bank of England (Goodhart and Crockett 1970) and by other researchers (Fisher 1968, Laidler and Parkin 1970) demonstrated the existence of a stable short run demand relationship which was sensitive — but not unduly so — to variations in interest rates and applicable, with hardly any modification, to all of the then commonly employed definitions of money (M1, M2 and M3). This empirical work is examined in the next chapter. Here we note that by fitting in as it did with comparable evidence for other countries, it reinforced the case as argued by monetarists for using the money supply, or its rate of growth, as an indicator of (or target for) monetary policy.

At any rate, it is a matter of record that from the late 1960s the monetary authorities increasingly emphasised monetary aggregates in their policy statements (Bank of England 1971a). From their viewpoint the switch of emphasis to aggregates like M3, which embrace the liabilities of all banks, meant that the class of bank could be ignored in future policy deliberations. By focusing upon the total of bank liabilities, the composition of bank assets between securities and loans took on less importance. But, overridingly, the demand for money relationship allowed the authorities to conceive of a method of monetary control which did not have to rely upon direct controls. The evidence suggested that higher interest rates led, *ceteris paribus*, to a reduction in the money supply. Accordingly, monetary policy objectives could be achieved via market mechanisms.

Reforms of 1971

The package of measures introduced in September 1971 and known as Competition and Credit Control (Bank of England 1974) can be thought of as falling into three parts. First, the most distorting of the controls were abolished. Quantitative restrictions upon bank advances were removed, and the cartel arrangements over clearing bank interest rates were abandoned. Second, while some controls remained, they were lightened in their incidence or extended to other institutions, or both. The minimum 8% cash reserve ratio became a 1.5% cash reserve requirement embracing just bankers' balances held at the Bank of England. The 28% liquid assets ratio changed in form to a 12.5% reserve asset ratio embracing bankers' balances, call money, bills and very short term bonds. Both special deposits and the reserve asset ratio were applied to all banks, and the latter was extended to finance houses (but at a lower rate). Third, there was a commitment to competition and market forces in the achievement of credit control objectives. 'Importance was now attached to the monetary aggregates; their rate of growth was to be controlled by the market instrument of interest rates' (Bank of England 1978).

As we have noted, the monetary aggregate which was preferred (M3) embraced all banks, but it was the means chosen to influence the aggregate that represented the important step. While direct controls remained the basic technique of credit control, what the Chief Cashier in 1971 called the 'problem [of] where to draw the line across the field of financial intermediaries' would continue to bedevil policy (Bank of England 1971b). In the new approach variations in interest rates were to exert a 'generalised influence on credit conditions' (now termed 'monetary conditions'). So long as policy continued to be operated in this 'non-discriminatory' fashion, all forms of intermediation should be governed by the same market forces. So long as the response of the different kinds of intermediation to interest rates is broadly similar across the spectrum, the operation of policy ought not to distort competition nor pose questions of equity. 'Where to draw the line' for the definition of monetary control should cease to be a problem, for the aggregates should provide a reliable guide to the behaviour of 'general liquidity'.

Policy since 1971 has been far from non-discriminatory (in this sense). Like the first experiment with interest rate control 20 years before, advances requests and interest rate ceilings (on retail deposits) were reintroduced within two years. Shortly afterwards, a new direct control (Supplementary Special Deposits) was introduced to reinforce the application of the interest rate weapon by imposing a rising marginal cash reserve requirement on the growth of banks' interest bearing liabilities from a base date. Continued reliance upon this technique (the 'corset'), which was really designed for temporary use, during each period of restrictive policy led the banks to find ingenious ways of inflating their balance sheets in anticipation of a period of policy restraint and of undertaking ways of winding down their balance sheets ('cosmetic' disintermediation) during its application (see Chapter 6). As in the 1960s, the controls became more distorting, less potent, and increasingly irksome to the authorities. The reforms of 1980 should be seen as a re-affirmation of the original aims of Competition and Credit Control: that, as far as possible, the special controls upon banks should be removed, not imposed upon other institutions, and the 'market instrument of interest rates' should regulate credit creation.

Reforms of 1980

Certainly, there are similarities in the composition of the measures introduced. First, the most distorting of the controls has been abolished — namely the Supplementary Special Deposits scheme. In addition, the reserve asset ratio is now seen to be redundant for control of interest rates. Worse, as we argue in Chapter 4, its existence alters the relationship between Treasury bill yields and other market rates in a way which makes control of the money supply more difficult. Consequently the ratio is being phased out and replaced by new prudential liquidity norms.[3] Second, credit controls are being applied more broadly. Policy statements give increasing emphasis to measures of liquidity (such as the officially designated PSL1 and PSL2 series) which embrace institutions such as the building societies, which are growing very rapidly (see table 1.1), as well as monetary aggregates which cover banks alone. Further, monetary aggregates like M3 are likely to be widened by the new Banking Act. There is a conviction that institutions competing for funds and which the Bank supervises under the Act, need to be treated equally for credit control and prudential requirements. If this reasoning is carried through, licensed deposit takers will be included with banks in the definition of the money supply and for the application of Special Deposits. Third, there is a commitment to market forces in the allocation of credit. Banking and financial activities in sterling can be externally produced in Euromarkets, free of domestic regulations. Exchange control regulations, which impede access to these markets, can be viewed as a form of protection to domestically located institutions (Davis and Lewis 1981). The removal of exchange controls (though clearly prompted in this case by other considerations) is thus a powerful competitive device, and as such has been welcomed in some quarters as a means of ensuring that future controls remain non-discriminatory.

As a result of these changes interest rates are virtually the sole remaining monetary instrument for achieving monetary control (the authorities also include fiscal policy). In view of the past experiences of interest rate controls, one must ask whether this instrument can bear the additional burdens which are to be placed upon it. Unlike the situation in 1971, there is no longer the same degree of confidence in the demand for money function. In Chapters 2 and 3, we seek to ascertain whether the authorities can rely upon the existence of a stable demand for money function and ask what can be expected from achievement of money supply targets.

Competition and Credit Control was inaugurated at a time when economic expansion was welcomed, and this obscured the difficulties of credit control which emerged subsequently. Now a policy of monetary restraint is the corner-stone of economic management. Because of concern for short run monetary management, the Bank of England is altering its existing procedures in money markets with the aim of letting market forces have a greater say in determining short term interest rates. The Bank's present and proposed methods are are examined in Chapter 4.

In response to the suspicion that control via interest rates may not be enough, the authorities are also experimenting with various systems of monetary base control. The viability of this technique of monetary control depends much upon the character of the banking system and the methods of intermediation employed. This is considered in Chapter 5 prior to a comparison of monetary base control and interest rate control in Chapter 6.

Notes to Chapter 1

1. Proposed new arrangements are set out in the following papers: Foreign currency exposure (1979), Bank of England, December. The measurement of liquidity (1980), Bank of England, March. The measurement of capital (1980), *Bank of England Quarterly Bulletin*, September.
2. *Monetary Control. A Consultation Paper by H M Treasury and the Bank of England* (1980), HMSO Cmnd 7858, March.
3. These decisions are outlined in Monetary control: next steps (1981) and The liquidity of banks (1981), both in *Bank of England Quarterly Bulletin*, March.

2

The Demand for Money

It is not surprising that much effort has been devoted to determining the form and stability of the demand for money function in Britain, as in other countries. The relationship is critical to a number of macro-economic models. In the IS/LM framework, for example, the interest elasticity of the demand for money governs the effectiveness of monetary policy, while a stable relationship is needed if monetary policy is to exert a predictable impact upon interest rates and income. Monetarists look to a stable demand for money function as the basis of the link between money and price inflation under floating exchange rates. Alternatively, with fixed exchange rates, the equation enables one to read off the implication of monetary policy for the balance of payments position.

Under certain conditions, the demand for money function may also be the basis of controlling the money supply. Encouraged by empirical investigations undertaken by its Research Department, the Bank of England has looked to the stability of demand for money functions as a means of controlling the money stock via interest rates. This empirical evidence was drawn predominantly from the 1960s. The discovery that these relationships may have altered substantially in the 1970s both undermines the basis of this policy and raises questions about the other aspects above. This chapter examines to what extent previously observed relationships between money, income and interest rates have been interrupted by events in the 1970s.

Theoretical Considerations

Theories of the demand for money developed by Keynes (1936), Baumol (1952), Tobin (1956, 1958) and Friedman (1956) are well known and need not be re-stated here — see Laidler (1977) for an excellent survey. These theories continue to form the basis of empirical work. Subsequent theoretical advances have not been entirely absent. In particular, the interrelationships between payment habits, inflation and the transactions demand for money have been thoroughly explored by Patinkin (1965), Niehans (1978) and Akerlof and Milbourne (1980). This newer work emphasises that both the timing of receipts and payments, and the terms of payment (credit) can be expected to adjust to the quantity of money, as well as the reverse. In consequence, the short run response of the transactions demand to movements of income and interest rates may be small. But, by and large, the substantial hypotheses embodied in the earlier work remain intact.

Three basic ideas are involved. First, since money is central to the payments mechanism in the economy, the amount that individuals and business firms wish to hold (M^*) varies directly with the flow of real income (y) either reflecting anticipated transactions or proxying for wealth. Second, because M^* refers to nominal money balances, the price level (P) is included as a scale variable to indicate variations in the purchasing power of money. Third, because money is only one among many forms in which wealth may be held and because balances held for transactions have an opportunity cost, desired balances can be expected to vary inversely with a vector of interest rates on relevant alternative assets $([r])$, and the expected rate of inflation $(\dot{p})$ relative to the own interest rate paid on money balances (r_M). These considerations lead to a relationship of the form:

$$M^* = f(P, y, [r], r_M, \dot{p}) \qquad (1)$$

Much work has been done to find the precise empirical counterparts of these theoretical variables by transforming actual magnitudes into expected variables, experimenting with various functional forms, and using different measures of the opportunity cost of holding money. On the latter, wealth-holders have a choice of holding money or a variety of financial and real assets — bills, bonds, equities and commodities. In an open economy, foreigners hold sterling in the form of bank deposits and other short term paper, while UK residents hold foreign currency claims in equivalent forms, so that interest rates on foreign securities also influence the demand for money. However, in most instances selection of one representative rate, such as the yield on consols (for long term securities) or local authority borrowing rates (for short term securities), has proven to be adequate. Similarly, while there are sound theoretical reasons to expect the inflation rate to influence the demand for money over and above that effect incorporated into nominal interest rates, the impact of $\dot{p}$ has frequently been seen to be taken up by the interest rate. With these simplications, (1) becomes

$$M^* = f(P, y, r, r_M) \tag{1a}$$

As a further simplification we may suppose that the demand function is unit elastic with respect to prices. This is on the grounds that transactors are concerned with the real purchasing power of money balances and that rational economic behaviour implies the absence of money illusion. On this basis, we obtain

$$M^*/P = f(y, r, r_M) \tag{2}$$

so that the dependent variable is desired *real* money balances. If we further suppose that the demand for real money balances is proportional to real income, nominal income can be used as the scale variable and (2) simplifies to

$$M^*/Y = f(r, r_M) \tag{3}$$

In this case the dependent variable is the desired ratio of money to income, i.e. the Cambridge 'k'. If (3) is inverted we have a *velocity function*, relating the desired income velocity of money to measures of the cost of holding money. All three functional relationships (1)–(3) have featured in the empirical work undertaken in Britain.

Empirical Studies Before 1971

In Britain as in the USA, research into the demand for money function proceeded at two levels, one concerned with an examination of long run trends, the other dealing with short run dynamics. For both sets of analyses, two implicit assumptions were made. One concerned the variable r_M which was omitted from all of the studies. Since the cost of holding money depends on the *difference* between market rates of interest (r) and the own rate (r_M), use of r alone is predicated on the assumption that the own rate adjusts sluggishly to market forces. Such rigidity was to be expected from the cartel arrangements which marked the clearing banks' interest rate setting prior to Competition and Credit Control. Second, desired money balances cannot be observed. The studies assumed, simply, equality of actual with desired balances, *viz:*

$$M = M^*, \quad \frac{M}{P} = \frac{M^*}{P}, \quad \frac{M}{Y} = \frac{M^*}{Y} \tag{4}$$

In fact, quite different behavioural assumptions are involved here. The equality of M with M^* implies that the nominal amount of money is determined by demand alone, rather than by some mixture of demand and supply. No such implication necessarily follows from the other equalities. Adjustment of M/P or M/Y to desired levels could result from movements in P or Y, as the case may be, as well as from M. These specifications allow for the possibility of the money supply being only partially determined by demand.

Long run studies of the demand for money were undertaken by Paish (1958, 1959), Dow (1958), Kavanagh and Walters (1966) and Laidler (1971). M2, defined as currency plus net deposits of the London clearing banks, is the most reliable series available for long run analysis and this was employed in all of the studies. Paish and also Dow (now an Executive Director of the Bank of England) presented graphical evidence of equation (3) in their evidence to the Radcliffe Committee. They showed the existence of a close relationship between the ratio of money to income and the long term bond rate for both pre- and post-war years. These results were confirmed with regression analysis in the other studies. Kavanagh and Walters found, with simple relationships of the kind used by Paish and Dow, that movements in interest rates were able to 'explain' 70% of the variations in the ratio of money to income from 1923 to 1961. With more general functions, like (1a), they estimated an income elasticity of demand for money of around unity (estimates varying from 0.96 to 1.1) and an interest rate elasticity of between −0.3 and −0.8. Given the length of the period covered (1880−1960), the studies suggested a much greater stability of the demand for money than many had thought existed. As Laidler noted, the demand for money function for Britain over the long run does not look very different from that for the United States.[1]

These investigations did not establish whether the relationships could be relied upon for shorter periods of time. For this purpose an examination of quarterly data was required. But it was soon found that sensible results depended upon introducing lags into the equations estimated. Substitution of expected for actual magnitudes in (1a) is one method of doing so, but quarterly data might also be expected to reflect lags in bringing nominal balances, real balances or the ratio of money to income to desired levels. Accordingly, the idea of 'partial adjustment' was incorporated: that people will not move to their desired long run money holding immediately, but will take time to do so, either through inertia or because it is too costly to move instantaneously.

With this additional hypothesis, the standard equation used in the Bank's empirical work (Goodhart and Crockett 1970) can be derived.[2] We rewrite (1a) as

$$M_t^* = a + bY_t + cr_t + u_t \tag{5}$$

where $Y = Py$ and u_t is a random error term, all variables being transformed to logarithms. Partial adjustment of 'short run' demand to changes in the determinants of 'long run' demand produces

$$M_t^{DS} - M_{t-1}^{DS} = \delta(M_t^* - M_{t-1}^{DS}) + v_t \tag{6}$$

where M^{DS} denotes the 'short run' demand. The system is again closed by assuming equality of actual with desired balances, now in the form

$$M = M^{DS} \tag{7}$$

That is, a passive supply response reconciles the short run demand to long run desired levels. Combining (5)–(7) we obtain the usual short run demand for money function

$$M_t = \alpha_0 + \alpha_1 Y_t + \alpha_2 r_t + \alpha_3 M_{t-1} + w_t \tag{8}$$

where $\alpha_0 = \delta a$, $\alpha_1 = \delta b$, $\alpha_2 = \delta c$, $\alpha_3 = 1 - \delta$, and $w_t = \delta u_t + v_t$. In (8), all fluctuations in the nominal money stock are assumed to be attributable to changes in the demand for money, these being induced by variables on the right hand side of the equation.

Any individual may acquire or dispose of money balances in the manner indicated in (8), but this need not imply that aggregate money balances, especially the broad M3 definition, adjust in the same way. However, those who investigated the short run demand for money function in Britain on the basis of an argument like that exemplified in equations (5)–(8) could appeal to certain features of the institutional arrangements in the 1960s as providing some support for their approach. In particular, with a fixed rate of exchange and interest rate pegging policies, transactors were afforded some implicit guarantees about their freedom to exchange money for bonds or foreign securities on demand; to this extent (and the account is obviously a highly stylised one) the argument runs that the amount of money actually in existence is determined by *demand*, as excess supplies can be instantaneously liquidated without repercussions for the arguments of the demand function. By this token, the maintained view (equations (5)–(8)) is all very well for the 1960s when these institutional arrangements prevailed but is clearly unsatisfactory for the 1970s. This dichotomy is probably rather too sharp, anyhow, for the institutional arrangements were never in fact quite so clear cut as earlier implied (foreign exchange controls flanked the fixed exchange rate, and interest rates were never pegged outright); and, since money is a temporary abode of purchasing power and an ideal buffer stock, accumulations of money reflecting a halfway house in a portfolio reallocation do represent a discrepancy between desired and actual holdings. How long this discrepancy exists and the means by which it is removed become vital questions. By assuming the nominal money stock to be demand-determined, the answers to these questions were effectively pre-judged by the researchers.

While monetary policy was thus assumed to be primarily accommodating in the demand studies, the results encouraged the view that it might possess the potential for more active use. As judged by the plausibility of the coefficients obtained and the goodness-of-fit statistics, the demand for money appeared to be stably related to income and interest rates, the latter providing a control mechanism so that 'appropriate' levels of the money supply could be achieved by market forces within a more competitive financial system (Goodhart 1979). From the Bank's equations, these appropriate levels of M3 required that this aggregate expand at a more rapid rate than income to allow for an income elasticity of demand for money greater than unity (nearer to 2 in some of the evidence, see Price 1972).

A rapid growth of M3 was permitted after the reform of credit control in 1971, especially in 1973, for this and a variety of other reasons, some of which — like allowance for a growth in bank intermediation ('re-intermediation') — were also associated with views about the demand for money. (Gowland (1978) gives an excellent insider's view to the Bank's thinking.) Unfortunately, attempts to explain this growth of the money supply in terms of the normal demand functions have met with little success (Artis and Lewis 1974).

Research Since 1971

Table 2.1 summarises the research into the short run demand for money function since 1971, including the Bank's work as a benchmark. In our earlier analysis of the demand for money (Artis and Lewis 1974 and 1976), we presented evidence which suggested to us that demand functions of the conventional kind broke down for both definitions of money after 1971. Subsequent research has confirmed our judgment about M3, but there is less agreement about M1. Coghlan (1978a, 1980a) in particular argues that there is reasonable

Table 2.1 Summary of Studies of the Short Run Demand for Money Function in Britain

Study	Data	Income Variable	Interest Rate	Long run Elasticity with respect to Income	Interest Rate	Comments
A. NARROW MONEY, M1						
Goodhart and Crockett (1970)	1955(3)–69(3)	GDP	3mo LA Consol	1.25 1.09	−1.05 −0.80	
Hacche (1974)	1963(4)–72(4)	TFE	3mo LA Consol	0.70	−0.06 −0.21	
Artis and Lewis (1976)	1963(2)–73(1)	GDP	Consol	1.24	−0.66	Instability in 1971
Hamburger (1977)	1963(1)–70(4)	GDP	3mo Eurodollar	0.67	−1.07	No adjustment lags in model. Instability in 1972
Coghlan (1978a)	1964(1)–76(4)	TFE	3mo LA	1.01	−0.30	Complex adjustment lags. No instability
Mills (1978a)	1963(2)–74(4)	TFE	3mo LA Consol	0.39 0.92	−0.24 −0.45	
Boughton (1979)	1963(2)–77(3)	GDP	3mo LA	1.32	−0.51	Instability in 1971
Rowan and Miller (1979)	1963(2)–77(2)	TFE	3mo Eurodollar	0.56	−0.08	Instability in 1971–73 period

B. BROAD MONEY, M3

Study	Period		Interest rate			Notes
Goodhart and Crockett (1970)	1963(2)–69(3)	GDP	3mo LA	1.41	−0.21	(a) Personal Sector
			Consol	1.54	−0.51	(b) Corporate sector
Price (1972)	1964(1)–70(4)	GDP	Consol	(a) 2.29	−0.30	
			3mo LA	(b) 2.77	−0.36	
Hacche (1974)	1963(4)–72(4)	TFE	3mo LA	(i) *	*	(i) Standard equation
				(ii) 1.00	−0.25	(ii) Inserting interest rate variable for shift after 1971
Artis and Lewis (1976)	1963(2)–73(1)	GDP	Consol	(1) 3.89	−1.46	(1) Standard equation
				(2) 1.21	−0.34	(2) Interest rate adjustment equation
Mills (1978a)	1963(2)–74(4)	TFE	3mo LA	*	*	Instability evident
			Consol	11.29	−3.74	
Boughton (1979)	1963(2)–77(3)	GDP	Consol	*	*	Instability evident

Notes:

* Coefficient on lagged dependent term exceeds unity.

GDP = Gross Domestic Product

TFE = Total Final Expenditure

3mo LA = 3 month Local Authority Rate

evidence for the existence of a stable M1 equation with theoretically plausible coefficients.

The other studies summarised in table 2.1 would suggest that some caution is in order, for we are not alone in finding evidence of instability in M1 equations in the 1971–3 period — see Hamburger, Boughton, and Rowan and Miller. More seriously, there are disturbing differences between the studies in the particular estimates. Long run income elasticities vary from 0.39 to 1.32 and an equivalent sized range exists for the estimated interest rate elasticities.

Coghlan's data sample ended in 1976. Table 2.2 sets out features of equations containing the same explanatory variables, but estimated for later periods. The similarity of the underlying long run parameters with those of Coghlan's (income elasticities of around unity and interest rate elasticities of about −0.30) is suggestive of reasonable stability in the M1 function after 1971. However, these equations are less successful in their short run properties and do not pick up sharp changes in the rate of growth of M1. Specifically, the first equation *underpredicts* the increase in M1 in 1978–9, while the second equation (which includes these observations in its data sample) *overpredicts* subsequently in 1980 when M1 declined more sharply than would be expected from past responses to interest rates. To the extent that customers now react to interest rate changes more forcefully than in the past, the measured interest rate elasticity may now be too small.

Support for this line of reasoning comes from the instability which has been evident recently in demand functions for narrow definitions of money in other countries, notably in Canada and the United States (Federal Reserve Bank of New York 1980). The instability has been attributed to financial innovations, as business firms use cash management systems to economise on transactions balances, and households transfer funds into interest-bearing time and savings accounts. Once it is recognised that payment habits are endogenous to financial developments, it is not difficult to envisage that the scale of interest rate movements experienced in the second half of the 1970s may have elicited more rapid changes in payments practices. This is an area which could repay further investigation in the UK.

THE DEMAND FOR MONEY

Table 2.2 Estimates of the Demand for Money Function M1[a]

Period of Estimation	TFE at Constant Prices (X)	Regression Coefficients for:			R^2	D.W.
		Price Deflator for TFE (P)	Interest[b] Rate (R)	Lagged Dependent Variable		
1964(1)–78(2)	0.416 X_0 (3.44)	0.623 P_{-1} (2.55)	−0.055 R_0 (5.34)	0.767 (11.87)	.998	2.54
	−0.185 X_{-3} (1.58)	−0.552 P_{-2} (1.39)				
		0.332 P_{-3} (0.48)				
		−0.088 P_{-4}				
Long Run Elasticities	*0.99*	*1.35* (0.38)	*−0.24*			
1964(1)–79(4)	0.332 X_0 (2.82)	0.580 P_{-1} (2.43)	−0.046 R_0 (4.70)	0.863 (16.43)	.998	2.57
	−0.193 X_{-3} (1.66)	−0.498 P_{-2} (1.25)				
		−0.045 P_{-3} (0.12)				
		0.081 P_{-4} (0.37)				
Long Run Elasticities	*1.01*	*0.86*	*−0.34*			

Source: Part of continuing research in the Bank of England, unpublished estimates by J.M. Trundle
Notes: a. Data are quarterly and all variables are measured in natural logarithms
       b. Local authority three month rate

It was the belief that bank customers react to high nominal interest rates by switching funds from sight deposits into interest bearing time deposits, without altering the total to the same extent, which in part led to M3 being favoured for policy use in the first place. Yet the problems with the M1 equation are of a much lesser order than for the M3 equation, as all attempts to update beyond 1971 the type of equations used by Goodhart and Crockett have proven unsuccessful. Those which have been published are summarised in Section B of table 2.1 and there are many unpublished equations which are characterised by the same flaw. This is that the equations are dominated by the autoregressive structure, so that the coefficient α_3 on lagged money balances in (8) is close to or exceeds unity, resulting in estimates of the long run elasticities which are theoretically implausible or which cannot be calculated. The breakdown is much the same for all M3 equations irrespective of whether the dependent variable is in nominal terms or expressed as real or real *per capita* balances; the same is found to be true for functions which incorporate as arguments short term rates, long term rates, foreign rates, dividend yields, and measures of the variance of bond yields. Even equations with generalised functional forms or more sophisticated lags fail after 1971. As a consequence, use of a demand equation for M3 has become discredited and it has been quietly dropped from all of the major macroeconomic models of the UK economy.

As well as documenting this failure, two of the studies (Hacche, Artis and Lewis) attempt to take matters further within the constraint of single equation methods. Their explanations revolve around the two assumptions implicit in earlier work (see pp. 12–15 above): one to the effect that variations in the 'own' rate of interest (r_M) could no longer be ignored in the new competitive environment, the other that the conditions of Competition and Credit Control (or more correctly the lack of credit control) gave rise to movements in the money supply in excess of demand, so violating the assumption $M^* = M$ (or $M^{DS} = M$). As a third alternative, which is necessarily residual, we are left with instability as a characteristic of the demand for money, either because of a Radcliffean view that there is no stable relationship short of

'general liquidity' (*Radcliffe Report* 1959) or because of
'Goodhart's Law' — that any empirical regularity is likely to
prove unreliable when it is leaned upon for policy purposes
(Goodhart 1979).[3]

Investigations by the Bank of England initially favoured an
interpretation along the lines of the first or third of these
explanations. With the abolition of the interest rate cartel,
banks competed more aggressively for interest-bearing deposits,
especially for large 'wholesale' deposits drawn from the
parallel money markets. By offering more competitive interest
rates on these deposits, they could make 'money' more
attractive to hold, so inducing a process of 're-intermediation'
of business originally lost to the parallel markets. It seems
only reasonable to expect the 'own rate' on money to be
more significant in these conditions. Subsequently, allowance
was made for it both in the Bank's study (by Hacche) and in
our own work.

Nevertheless, equations which include measures of the own
rate of money still do not provide satisfactory explanations
of the 1971—3 experience. The coefficients with 1970s data
included differ markedly from those derived from the 1960s
and it is possible to get a reasonable looking equation over
both periods only by including variables which are akin to a
proxy for a break in the relationship around 1971. There are,
admittedly, statistical difficulties in measuring the own rate
relevant for the 're-intermediation' process, and in capturing
the 'merry-go-round' or 'round-tripping' experience, whereby
relativities between deposit rates and loan rates altered such
that it was profitable for corporations to borrow from banks
and acquire deposits (especially CDs for which the identity
of the holder is unknown). But experiments with demand for
money functions where money is defined as M3, excluding
CDs, were no more successful.

Accordingly, our own investigations proceeded onto the
second of the explanations, querying the presumption of
earlier work that the economy was always effectively 'on the
demand curve'. Whereas previous studies treated the money
supply as responding to the determinants of demand with
a lag, the conditions of Competition and Credit Control seem
more likely to have reversed this presumption. Thus the

release of bank lending controls in 1971, changes of tactics in gilt-edged markets and the size of the budget deficit in 1972 and 1973 all offer reasons why one might conclude that the stock of money was not determined by the ongoing demand but rather in excess of it. Whilst individuals would move, possibly with a lag, to get rid of excess holdings, under floating exchange rates the dissipation takes time and is likely to involve adjustments to interest rates, expenditures and prices along the way.

Our 1976 article sought to pursue this line of reasoning by adopting as an initial hypothesis the position that the demand for money had remained stable, but that variations in supply conditions were responsible for a marked disequilibrium and excess supply of money, which gave the misleading appearance of a breakdown in the demand for money. In the first set of experiments we fitted functions with M/Y as the dependent variable, so as to allow for some adjustment of income to the excess supply, and also with variables to allow for supply shocks, especially from the release of advances requests. These 'supply' variables appear to have exerted some impact upon the growth of the money supply independently of the variables representing money demand. With the second set of experiments, we explored the idea that the disequilibrium was worked off, at least initially, via adjustments in the structure of interest rates. This assumption enabled us to estimate the parameters of the (long run) demand for money function underlying the reaction process. These parameters are set out in table 2.3 where it can be seen that they show less variability over the various time periods than those from the 'standard' equation. (It is noticeable also that the estimated income elasticity is much lower than the range estimated by Goodhart and Crockett, and Price).

While these initial results were encouraging to the idea that the demand function survived the initial phase after 1971, matters have rested there. The restoration of greater credit control since 1974 has thrown up data which are less easy to interpret, in similar vein, as a disequilibrium position of excess supply in the money market, and the equations do not predict well after 1974. And while the main thrust of our argument is to the effect that measurement of the demand for money

Table 2.3 Estimates of the Long Run Elasticities of Parameters of the Demand for Money Function M3

Period of Estimation	Standard Equations		Interest Rate Equations	
	Income Elasticity	Interest Rate* Elasticity	Income Elasticity	Interest Rate* Elasticity
1963(2)–70(4)	1.18	−.28	1.22	−.37
1963(2)–71(4)	1.23	−.27	1.25	−.40
1963(2)–73(1)	3.89	−1.46	1.21	−.34

Source: Artis and Lewis (1976), Tables 2 and 7
Note: * The differential between the consol rate and the 'own rate' on money

has been tackled incorrectly, so that the behaviour of conventional single equation functions may not be indicative of instability of the 'true' demand function because of specification errors (see also Lewis 1978), this is far from establishing that there is stability post-1973. Despite this lack of evidence, the authorities have, almost as an act of faith, gone ahead and set money supply targets for M3 (and later £M3), an exercise which seems of doubtful value if the demand function really is inherently unstable or is subject to institutional change, the impact of which upon demand cannot be predicted in advance. In the remainder of this chapter we seek to ascertain whether there is evidence to suggest that a stable long run demand relationship for broad money exists, and whether this function can be relied upon for control of the money supply via interest rates.

Stability of Demand for Money

The original demand functions for M3 fitted by the Bank of England covered only 7 years of data, 1963 to 1969 (although equations for M1 and M2 examined 15 years of data). This period of time is hardly adequate to make judgments about the longer run stability of the demand for money function, as the authors acknowledged. Over these seven years, the money supply M3 increased by 53%. In the two years after Competition and Credit Control was introduced, M3 increased by 65%. It is easy to understand that the original functions could be overwhelmed by a disturbance of this magnitude. Functions fitted to a longer time period may enable us to put this episode and later experience into better perspective.

For a long run analysis we are unable to use any of the standard definitions, M1, £M3 or M3, since data are not available. Our analysis is confined to a money supply definition equivalent to the old M2, comprising currency in circulation outside of banks, plus sterling deposits of London clearing banks. As at the end of 1979, this magnitude constituted just under 80% of £M3. It can be argued, *pace* Goodhart and Crockett, that the liabilities of the non-clearing banks are less liquid than those of the clearing banks, so that their omission is justified on these grounds.

When supply shocks are present, use of real money balances (M/P) or the ratio of money to income (M/Y) as the dependent variable reinforces the expectation that we are measuring a demand function and not something else. Of the two, the latter is more general in allowing for adjustments in nominal balances, prices and real expenditures to occur in response to divergences of money holdings from desired levels. Its use does, however, constrain the income elasticity of demand for money to unity. An elasticity of this magnitude conflicts with the Bank's estimates for broad money based on the 1960s' data sample, but we have indicated that confidence in these estimates has been eroded by later experience. Our assumption of unitary elasticity, on the other hand, does correspond with an income elasticity of .96 estimated for the same definition by Kavanagh and Walters, and elasticities of .91 to 1.04 estimated for 1924 to 1977 by Smith (1978), although his definition of M2 differs from our data after 1970.

Use of the ratio of money to income in the exercise has a further advantage. It enables us to base an examination of the stability of the demand for money around the earlier analyses of Paish and Dow. Their data sample finished in 1957. Our objective, simply, is to see how well subsequent developments conform to their hypothesis.

We first replicated the data series these studies employed, taking into account recent revisions. The data are annual averages for the years 1920–57. As income we use GNP at factor cost, and the interest rate is the yield on 2.5% consols.[4]

Both Paish and Dow plotted the consol yield on one axis and on the other axis the Cambridge 'k', the ratio of money to income. Their scatter diagrams show a clear inverse relationship, with some displacement around the war years. We fitted an equation to the observations. The form of equation chosen was

$$\frac{M}{Y} = ar^b \quad \text{or} \quad \log \frac{M}{Y} = \log a + b \log r \qquad (9)$$

in which the variables are related linearly in logarithms. This equation produces a relationship between r and M/Y that looks much like the textbook Keynesian liquidity preference curve. (For later reference, we note that the equation is equivalent to a linear relationship between r and V, V being the velocity of money Y/M.) For the years 1920–57 the estimated equation is

$$\log M/Y = 4.718 - 0.584 \log r$$
$$R^2 = .52$$

The estimated interest rate elasticity of −.58 may be compared with the elasticity of −.55 estimated by Kavanagh and Walters. When the war years are omitted, the consol rate is able to 'explain' 73% of the variation in M/Y. While expressing the relationship with M/Y on the left hand side, we recognise that movements along a liquidity preference schedule can reflect both the response of desired balances to interest rates and the adjustments of interest rates to variations in the quantity of money relative to income. But if the longer run path of gilt-edged rates is set by loanable funds, we may be entitled to see causation running in the manner specified.

In the second part of the exercise, we extended the data from 1957 through to 1979. These later data (indicated by stars) are plotted along with the original data (indicated by dots) in figure 2.1. The curve shown is drawn from the equation given in the previous paragraph; that is, estimated only on the basis of information for the 1920–57 period. Data points for the 1960s and for the first 3 years of the 1970s lie generally along the line. Indeed they are closer to the regression line than the points of the sample period! There is then a severe displacement such that observations for

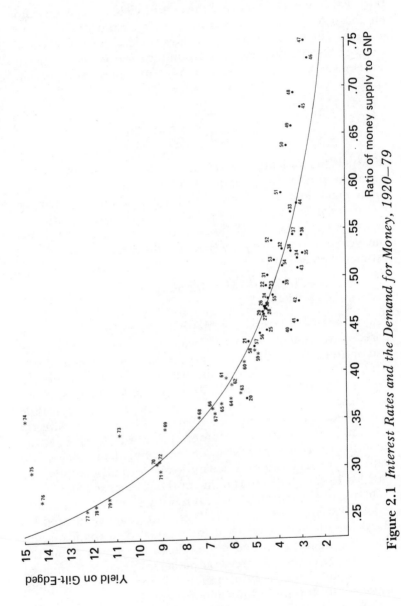

Figure 2.1 *Interest Rates and the Demand for Money, 1920–79*

THE DEMAND FOR MONEY

the years 1973 to 1976 lie well above the line. Following this disturbance, the data points for 1977–9 return almost exactly to the curve which, we emphasise, is predicted on the basis of a data sample ending 20 years before, in 1957.

While this evidence is suggestive of a considerable extent of long run stability in the demand for this definition of money (essentially M2), there remains the question of the preferred concept of money £M3 over shorter periods of time, and how we are to explain the marked divergences from the curve in the mid-1970s. Some perspectives on these points may be obtained from reference to figure 2.2, which shows the annual income velocity of £M3 in quarterly seasonally adjusted form from 1963. We fit a simple linear trend to the data prior to the institution of Competition and Credit Control (to the end of 1971, for banks were asked not to 'commence proceedings' before 1972). This trend is projected forward. There is a marked decline in velocity after 1971 but there is a return to the earlier trend around 1976.

This trend line could be the result of several factors, either singly or combined, namely: (i) an income elasticity of demand for money of *less than* unity; (ii) rising trend of interest rates; (iii) upward revisions to inflation expectations not incorporated into (ii); (iv) changes in payment practices or some other factors, correlated with time. Of these, the first is clearly contrary to the results of past research on the demand for M3 or £M3 and is ignored, although we note that if the income elasticity *exceeds* unity, the other factors must exert an influence strong enough to counteract a declining velocity as real income grows over time. If, on the other hand, we assume an income elasticity of unity and attribute the upward trend of velocity to rising interest rates, the long run interest rate elasticity of £M3 implied is −0.43 for the consol rate and −0.46 for the differential between the consol rate and the 'own' rate on money. These values seem plausible in view of past research, and if we accept this interpretation there is the advantage of not having to resort to the more complex factors implied by (iii) and (iv).

What of the displacement from the trend after 1971? Here there are two main contenders. One is the Treasury view which associates the disturbance with 'institutional changes

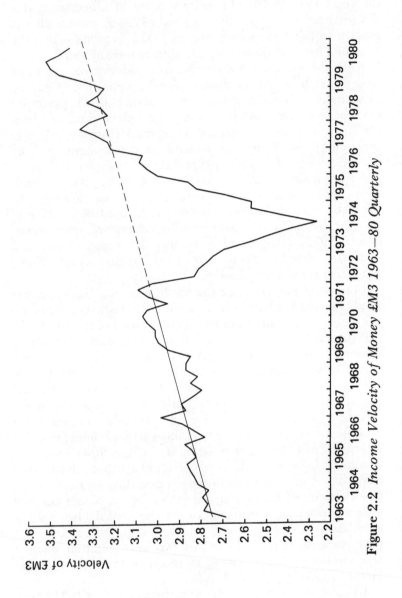

Figure 2.2 *Income Velocity of Money £M3 1963–80 Quarterly*

in the banking system' brought about by the Competition
and Credit Control reforms (*Economic Progress Report,* July
1980). Factors like the competitive bidding for interest
bearing deposits, roundtripping via Certificates of Deposit
(CDs), and a greater volatility of bond prices featured in our
earlier work (Artis and Lewis 1976), but as we have said cannot
account entirely for the experience. One factor that we did
not (indeed could not) allow for is that the process of 're-
intermediation', set in train by the reforms, raised the *non*
interest service flow attached to bank deposits by an amount
sufficient for desired balances to exceed their former levels
by the extent to which velocity is below trend. This explanation would then look to the operation of the corset after
December 1973 as reversing the process (disintermediation
producing a rise in velocity). Two comments can be made of
this argument. While not denying it as a possible contribution,
we doubt that it can be a major factor. It would seem entirely
fortuitous, to say the least, if the reversal of re-intermediation
resulted in velocity returning to exactly the same trend.
Second, while many of the institutional changes increased
actual deposit balances, whether they simultaneously increased
desired balances by an equal amount is an entirely different
matter. Unlike the Treasury, we do not accept that 'the
demand for money must necessarily be equal to the stock in
circulation'. Because of the proviso inserted, we disagree less
with the statement that 'the process of monetary control, at
least over a period of years, can be described indifferently as
control of the supply of money or control of the demand'
(*Economic Progress Report, ibid*).

Once the possibility of disequilibrium is accepted, the
second explanation can proceed. Variations in reserve requirements and other institutional changes contributed initially to
a disequilibrium between money supply and demand. Further
sources of new supply from government budget deficits and
the Bank's abolition of controls upon bank advances per-
petuated the cycle. In 1974, we estimated (conservatively)
that by mid-1973 the supply of M3 may have exceeded
demand by 62% (Artis and Lewis 1974). The extent of the
supply disturbance was misread by the authorities because
they believed in an income elasticity of demand of about 2,

so that the money stock should increase much faster than income, and because they could not (and in some cases still cannot) break away from the idea that the nominal money supply must necessarily be demand-determined. If, as our results suggest, the underlying demand function remained reasonably stable, the changes in the supply of money must either be dissipated through portfolio reallocations which eventually reduce the money supply or instead result in one or more of the arguments of the demand function for nominal balances changing in order for equilibrium in the money market to be restored. In the latter case, the discrepancy between actual and desired money holdings would be expected to result in adjustments to interest rates, the flow of expenditures and thus output and prices until the ratio of money to income, or velocity, is brought to the desired path.

Under the second interpretation then, the failure of the demand for broad money to fit during the 1970s is attributed to a supply shock which threw the private sector off its desired equilibrium path. While the disturbance persisted and until the adjustment processes began to catch up, we should expect the velocity of money to fall. By a combination of a slower growth of the money supply and rising prices and incomes, we should then expect the velocity of money to rise until levels traced out by the trend of interest rates are attained. This explanation is readily able to explain why velocity exhibited a tendency to return to its underlying trend.

Whichever of these explanations is favoured (and we see no reason why they cannot be combined), some things can be agreed upon. All of our tests point to there being some underlying longer run stability of the demand for broad money. Although we do not subscribe to the income elasticity of demand being greatly in excess of unity (if at all), we do find evidence, both direct and indirect, of an interest rate elasticity not much different from those found in the Bank's original studies. These studies, we recall, were instrumental in leading to the Competition and Credit Control reforms by allowing for management of the course of the monetary aggregates through interest rates. As the Governor has described it, the essential logic of monetary control since 1971 rests on the interest rate elasticity of the demand for money (Bank of

England 1978). Where does this now leave the idea of controlling the money supply via demand in the wake of the '1980 reforms', in which interest rates are again to be the major control variable?

Short Run Control

With two provisos the Treasury view of matters outlined above does at least allow for the possibility of short run monetary control by means of effecting movements along a demand for money curve. One proviso is that 'institutional change' does not recur as the banking system is de-regulated. The second proviso concerns the behaviour of interest rates. When we are dealing with the short run behaviour of the demand for M3 (or £M3) we need to pay more regard to changes in the alignment of bank interest rates to market interest rates. These rates can no longer be sub-sumed under the behaviour of market rates, nor can the difference between them be expected to alter only slowly over time. Bank time deposits, included in M3, bear interest rates which are determined by the banks in competition with other institutions. Thus the interest rates which govern the public's demand for these deposits are bank deposit rates *relative* to rates on competing market assets. It is these differentials which are relevant to control via demand.

Since the terms offered by banks on wholesale deposits are unknown, being in the form of special deals, the calculation of the 'own' rate on interest bearing deposits cannot be a direct one. We broke down the interest bearing part of M3 into five components with which it seemed feasible to associate a uniform rate of interest, either the rate known to be effective or the rate on what seemed the nearest competitive paper. The components (and associated rate) are: (a) retail sterling deposit accounts at Deposit Banks and Discount Houses (London Clearing Bank, 7-day deposit rate); (b) wholesale sterling deposit accounts at Deposit Banks (Interbank, one month rate); (c) sterling deposit accounts and public sector accounts at other banks (Local Authority, 7-day rate); (d) non-sterling accounts at other banks and non-sterling

Certificates of Deposit (Eurodollar, 3-month rate); (e) sterling CDs at all banks (sterling CD rate). A weighted average of these rates of interest was then taken, using the relative values of the components as weights. The result, termed the 'time deposit rate', is graphed in figure 2.3.

If the assets which compete with bank deposits are short term paper (Treasury bills, local authority), then the differential does not change much in response to policy aimed at monetary control and exercised by variations in Bank rate (MLR). If the key portfolio choice is between holding long term assets like gilts and short term liquid assets, of which bank deposits are the major component, then the differential can behave perversely. Referring to figure 2.3, we see that in 1973, 1976 and 1978–80 when the authorities sought to restrain monetary growth, the time deposit rate increased relative to long term rates, indicated by the yield on consols, as actions undertaken via the discount market succeed in levering up short term rates, including those on bank deposits. The result is that the demand for money probably *increased* in these periods of monetary restriction.

The significance of this result for monetary control depends much upon what monetary variable is considered important in transmitting monetary policy to the real sector (i.e. money supply, interest rates, or 'monetary disequilibrium') and the extent to which the authorities are able to influence, by asset side transactions, the processes by which the money supply adjusts to demand. (With the former, we note that interest rates are, overall, higher and this should exert some restraint upon expenditures. With the latter, the addition to demand could result in an excess demand for money with similar restraint upon expenditures).

But in an environment in which transactors are able to satisfy their increased demand for bank deposits by transactions on the asset side of banks' balance sheet (for example, advances), the money supply M3 can in fact be inflated by measures intended to reduce it. Indeed, the belief that this was occurring led to the introduction of the Supplementary Special Deposits weapon (the 'corset'). It was a reserve requirement on marginal funds levied at an increasing marginal rate. By raising the marginal cost of funds to the banks,

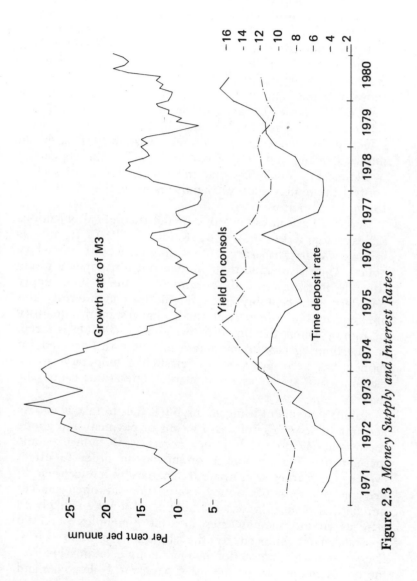

Figure 2.3 *Money Supply and Interest Rates*

it sought to prevent them from bidding for deposits and raising deposit interest rates relative to interest rates on advances and gilt-edged securities. (We discuss the operation of the corset in Chapter 6).

The general problem for the authorities is that the interest rate differential necessary for control via the demand side is not amenable to policy control. This was foreseen by David Laidler in 1973. Laidler argued that in a competitive banking system the fluctuation of bank deposit rates in line with those on competing assets would offset the tendency of the demand for money to vary with market interest rates. He saw this competition for funds as making monetary policy more effective by reducing the interest elasticity of both the money demand and the LM curves. However, this conclusion overlooks the possibility that the authorities might seek to control the money supply by movements within the demand for money function.

Here we have in essence one of the theoretical objections against monetarism raised by Kaldor in 1970. It runs as follows. Monetarists argue the importance of monetary policy. They also argue that the demand for money is insensitive to interest rates. If so, control of the money supply founders. Unacceptably large fluctuations in interest rates are required to effect even small changes in the quantity of money when the liquidity preference schedule is steep. In the limiting case of monetarism, where the demand for money has zero interest rate elasticity, monetary policy cannot work at all, as open market operations cannot be made!

Kaldor's argument is ingenious, but it fails to take adequate account of money's role as a means of payment and abode for purchasing power. It is not necessary to induce people 'permanently' to economise on money in order to effect every open market sale, nor is it necessary to induce them to become hoarders of money every time an open market purchase is made. Rather, the holding of money is likely to arise as an intermediate step in a more complex portfolio re-arrangement induced by the alteration to bond prices. Every non-barter transaction in a monetary economy involves the use of money as the means of payment. Unless sales and purchases are strictly synchronised in both timing and value, transactions necessarily involve holding purchasing power temporarily in monetary form (Friedman's concept of money as a temporary abode of purchasing power).

This distinction between a temporary and a more permanent holding of money means that money can come into existence, or be extinguished, without an accompanying and immediate movement along the 'long run' demand curve. Transactors can be forced 'off' the aggregate demand curve as the supply curve shifts independently of demand. This is because people do not refuse money, due to its special functions, even though the additions to their stock cause their holdings to be out of line with their underlying demand. So long as the underlying demand curve is reasonably stable in the face of the shift in supply, the resulting disequilibrium will have effects more broadly in the economy.

It is this 'monetary disequilibrium' idea, which can be traced back to our own work cited above and that of Jonson (1976) and Coghlan (1978b), which provides the theoretical basis of (the Bank's version of) the present 'supply side' approach to monetary control — a system designed to get around problems of short run control via demand. Once longer run stability of the demand for money is accepted instead, for this is crucial, the remaining questions are how shifts in supply are engineered in the approach and what consequences follow for the economy from these money supply 'targets'. These questions form the basis of the next two chapters.

Notes to Chapter 2

1. This similarity forms the basis of Friedman and Schwartz's forthcoming volume. See Friedman (1972, 1980) for preliminary results.
2. For an analysis and critique of this work the reader is referred to Courakis (1978) and Hendry and Mizon (1978).
3. See also Kaldor (1970) for views along the same lines. In a later letter to *The Times*, Dr Goodhart noted facetiously that influence of 'Murphy's Law' could also not be ignored — that if anything can go wrong, it will.
4. Information on data sources can be obtained from the authors.

3

Monetary Targets

As in many other countries, monetary policy in Britain has been framed increasingly in terms of the behaviour of monetary aggregates. Interest in the monetary aggregates began in the late 1960s under the stimulus not only of monetarist writings but also of an agreement reached with the IMF in 1967 because of Britain's international borrowings. This agreement saw the setting of targets for domestic credit expansion (DCE), which is the increase in M3 arising from domestic sources (a formal definition is given in Chapter 4). The IMF's concern was with the balance of payments. It was assumed that if DCE fell short of the increase in money demanded, then this shortfall would be made up with money from foreign sources, i.e. by way of an increase in international reserves necessarily involving an improvement in the balance of payments (under a fixed exchange rate). Conversely, and this was the major worry, if DCE outstripped the increase in money demand, the excess would result in a balance of payments deficit.[1] The practice of announcing anticipated DCE, later supplemented with statement of the expected increase in the money supply M3, continued until the reforms of 1971.

Competition and Credit Control, as we have seen, was designed around control of monetary aggregates, yet the institution of announcing 'targets' lapsed in 1972. An accelerating rise in the money stock was permitted because it was believed (wrongly it would seem) that the income elasticity of demand for money greatly exceeded unity. Although confidence in that belief quickly crumbled as demand for money functions began to exhibit marked instability, it was difficult to ascertain to what extent the factors which swelled M3 were matched by equal increases in the demand for money, in the light of the more competitive posture adopted by the banks as a result of the 1971 reforms. As the expansion of the money supply continued into 1973 it became increasingly obvious that monetary growth was 'excessive' under any criteria and that action had to be taken on the 'supply' side to constrain it. The need for this policy was later rationalised on the grounds that changes on the asset side of the banks' balance sheets (especially the surge in bank lending in 1972–3) had forced the growth of bank liabilities away from their usual relationship with nominal incomes and interest rates, as summarised in demand for money functions. On this disequilibrium view of the money market, it was not clear that the resulting money supply increases were demanded, but it was certainly true that they were 'supplied'.

From the end of 1973 attention was refocused upon the behaviour of the monetary aggregates in policy formulation. Initially a target growth rate of M3 was an internal aim of the Bank. By the second half of 1974, the growth rate of M3 had fallen below 10% per annum (from a rate in excess of 25% per annum 6 months before) and a 10% per annum growth was not approached again until 1976 (see figure 2.3). Renewed concern about the behaviour of the monetary aggregates led the Chancellor of the Exchequer in July 1976 publicly to declare an M3 target for the financial year 1976–7 of 12%. A ceiling on DCE was later set in December 1976 as a precondition for an IMF loan. Targets for DCE and target ranges for the money supply (now £M3) were set for 1977–8 and 1978–9. A further refinement was added in October 1978 when the practice of rolling the target forward every six months was adopted. Since 1978–9 only targets for £M3 have been declared (although other aggregates ranging from M1 through to wide measures of private sector liquidity are monitored closely) and, as part of the government's (1980) *Medium Term Financial Strategy* were set for the whole period up to 1983–4. Table 3.1 sets out past targets and the actual outcomes.

Table 3.1 Monetary Targets in the UK

		M3/£M3		DCE (£ billion)	
	Target (annual growth rate)	Result	Amount £ billion	Target	Result
1976–7	12	10.7	2.8	9.0	4.9
1977–8	9–13	16.4	6.2	7.7	3.8
1978–9	8–12	10.9	5.3	6.0	7.4
Oct. 1978–Oct. 1979	8–12	13.3	6.4	–	9.5
June 1979–Oct. 1980	7–11	17.2	12.1	–	18.4
Feb. 1980–April 1981	7–11	20.2*	11.3*	–	15.3*

* to February 1981

Role of Monetary Targets

Since the monetary aggregates are not objectives which matter for their own sakes, it must be asked why they feature at all in the formulation of policy. Monetary policy can be thought of as a process involving at one end the *instruments* of policy (e.g. open market operations) and at the other the *ultimate objectives* (or goal variables) of policy (inflation, output and employment, and the balance of payments). Between these two sets stand *intermediate variables* whose values respond to the setting of the instruments and which, in turn, either influence or provide an indication of the behaviour of the ultimate objectives. In a complex financial system, the 'thrust' of monetary policy instruments proceeds toward the policy objectives by a transmission process which successively incorporates a number of financial influences as the effects span out from the Bank of England to the discount houses, the banking system and other financial intermediaries. Actions by the authorities in terms of the instruments, such as altera-tions to MLR, the discounting of bills, open market operations in gilt-edged securities and Treasury bills, calls for and releases of Special Deposits, lack in themselves a common scale, upon which they can be aggregated. An intermediate variable is intended to solve this index number problem and to indicate how well the financial system is responding to the policy instruments. At the same time, the appropriateness of the authorities' response to the (mis)behaviour of the ultimate objectives can more readily be judged.

Interest rates have traditionally performed this function (although they have frequently been supplemented by other intermediate targets e.g. bank lending). Indeed, interest rates have probably done so for at least 120 years (Congdon 1980b). The traditional instruments used by the Bank of England are Bank rate (now MLR) and market operations in bills (discounting and lately the bill tender). These were employed to induce a structure of short term interest rates sought for balance of payments requirements or latterly for aggregate demand. Given this continuity in the Bank's operational procedures over so many years, the switch from interest rates to the use of monetary aggregates as intermediate targets might seem to be a radical departure from past strategies. It is not, because interest rates still feature in the Bank's strategy. They are now a step or *operational target* in achieving the money supply target. In effect, with the switch to emphasis upon monetary aggregates, the Bank grafted an additional intermediate step into formal operational procedures, thereby retaining continuity with traditional strategies. (These strategies are examined in Chapter 4).

Unlike some other central banks, the Bank has never regarded the money supply as so special that its control should be the sole focus of monetary policy. A money supply target has been chosen partly on tactical grounds, because interest rates are considered less reliable in periods of (variable) inflation as indicators. In the Governor's words:

> What swung the argument in favour of choosing a quantity rather than a price as the best indicator of the thrust of monetary policy was the acceleration of inflation. . . . We can, if we like, think of the nominal interest rate as having an 'expected inflation' component and a 'real' interest element. But we can never observe expectations, which are in any case likely both to differ from person to person, and to be volatile. The real rate of interest is an abstract construct. This has made it very difficult to frame the objectives of policy in terms of nominal interest rates. (Bank of England 1978).

For example, Bank rate rose from 5% in June 1972 to 13% in September 1973 — presumably a sharp tightening of policy

— yet with hindsight, inflation expectations are thought to have risen by even more over the same period, implying an easing in the stance of monetary policy (Foot 1981).

Implicit in these arguments is the hypothesis that what matters for expenditure decisions such as investment, is the expected real rate of interest, i.e. the nominal rate of interest after allowance for the expected rate of change of prices over the period of repayment although, given the usual form of loan contract — in which constant repayment schedules in nominal terms mean that the real burden of repayment is greater at the beginning of the contract — nominal rates may well have some significance in their own right. By the same token, however, interpreting the consequences of movements in the money supply for *real* demand also requires taking account of the way in which prices are changing (Artis 1978); it is only in terms of the inflation goal that the growth of the money supply is superior as an indicator.

On this interpretation, the switch to monetary aggregates in the 1970s is a reflection more of a change of emphasis within the goals of monetary policy, especially a concern with inflation. At the same time there was disillusionment with old remedies. Prices and incomes policies had been tried, but with mixed success. It would be incorrect to say they did not work (witness inflation in 1978), but their impact seemed to be merely temporary (see Lipsey and Parkin 1970, for one interpretation). Perhaps this was because of the form in which they were implemented or perhaps the accompanying stance of demand management was not appropriate. In any event, incomes policies became politically highly charged and a monetary rule for restraining wages became increasingly attractive, if only because of its relative novelty, and because the underlying environment had been altered by the transition to more flexible exchange rates.

Under the fixed exchange rate regime which operated prior to the 1970s, domestic prices in each country were linked ultimately to the course of world prices through the substitutability of domestic for internationally produced goods. In these circumstances, with expectations of inflation also geared to international developments, the conditions were conducive to monetary policy biting into the employment position, with the balance of payments indicating the extent to which domestic policies were out of line with those elsewhere. With the transition to more flexible exchange rates in the 1970s, the long run nexus which had previously existed between domestic and world prices was severed and the nature of price determination was altered.

Market forces in an economy are capable of determining *relative* prices but not the *absolute* price level. To determine absolute prices, some 'fixed point' is needed to tie down nominal magnitudes in the system. Previously, with a fixed exchange rate, it was the price of domestic money in terms of international money (with the quantity of money adjusting to guarantee external equilibrium). With flexible exchange rates, the price of domestic money relative to international money varies. Constraint upon variations in the quantity of money is needed for domestic price stability. In this more flexi-price environment, expectations of inflation might be expected both to be more volatile and to exert a larger influence upon wage and price setting mechanisms. Monetary growth targets thus seek to provide a 'peg' for these expectations, attempting to exert a direct influence upon their formation and substituting in the new environment for the 'anchor' which adherence to fixed exchange rates gave in the old (Lindbeck 1978).

If expectations of inflation are more attuned to domestic policies, the time span over which demand management policies can stimulate employment at the expense of prices might be shortened. That is, there could be a 'worsening' of the short run Phillips curve trade-off between inflation and unemployment. Policymakers have also added to this analysis the untested hypothesis — and we stress that this is all it is at this stage — that the process of inflation itself causes unemployment through the uncertainties and frictions which are introduced into private decision making. Faster inflation was seen to increase personal savings, depress business investment for long term projects, and worsen competitiveness of exports, where the exchange rate failed to compensate fully for wage and price trends in particular industries. These factors were seen to make for a coincidence of high inflation and high unemployment.[2] When all these views are put together the result is a major re-ordering of policy priorities in which the cure of inflation by adherence to monetary targets is seen to be a pre-condition for achievement of other economic goals, especially a sustained expansion of employment — an 'inflation first' strategy.

There is also a very practical reason why governments of all persuasions have wanted to appear to be paying attention to monetary developments. During the 1970s operators in bond and exchange rate markets seem to have been increasingly persuaded to the monetarist point of view. Pre-announced money supply targets seek to demonstrate that a greater medium term 'steadiness' in monetary management is to be pursued at the expense of 'Keynesian-style' short run interventions. In this way, governments have found it in their interests to accommodate to the prevailing psychology of markets. How this adds up globally, especially in terms of the employment objective, is less clear. There is a danger of countries competing with each other for status as strong currencies and responsible economic managers by adopting what are, essentially, 'beggar-thy-neighbour' monetary targets.

The argument that expectations can be favourably influenced by setting target rates of growth for monetary aggregates depends upon there being a stable relationship between the targeted aggregates and the ultimate goals of policy. In the long run, agents will expect prices and output to respond in a particular way to changes in the aggregate only if experience suggests that such a relationship exists, although in the short run the possibility that expectations may be 'rationally irrational' cannot be ruled out. Ignoring 'Goodhart's Law', it is sensible for the authorities to adopt a target for a monetary aggregate only if a reasonably stable relationship can be shown to exist between:

(a) the policy instruments and the monetary aggregate in question; and
(b) the monetary aggregate and the ultimate objective which the authorities wish to influence.

If the aggregate is either not controllable or has no predictable impact upon the policy goals, the value of setting a target must be questioned. Examination of these preconditions forms the basis of the remainder of this chapter and the next.

Effects of Monetary Policy

Since controlled experiments are ruled out, the only available source of information about the response of the goal variables to monetary policy is past experience. But economists are sharply divided over the appropriate way in which past experience should be assessed as a guide to policy making. The generally favoured *structural* approach explicitly outlines and, by the use of econometric techniques, estimates a complete macroeconomic model of the economy, incorporating all the interrelationships suggested by economic theory. An explicit statement is provided of the channels whereby changes in monetary policy are transmitted from instruments through the intermediate variables to the goal variables. Market operators and the financial press are more influenced by *reduced form* methods which make statistical comparisons of the time paths of goal variables and indicators of monetary policy (usually intermediate variables) in the hope of discovering information about the reliability of the response and the lags involved.

Neither approach is without faults. Structural models rely critically on the economic structure being modelled remaining stable over time (Lucas and Sargent 1979). It may be very difficult to estimate the structure of behaviour independently of the influence of policy upon it, and estimates which do not do so must necessarily succumb to instability as policy changes. Reduced form models, which deliberately eschew specification of specific channels and concentrate on the overall relationship via many mechanisms, may better survive structural change. Yet, as is well known, correlations do not establish causation. Goal variables reflect a variety of forces and by ignoring other variables, reduced form examinations may wrongly attribute their influence to monetary changes.

In our view this debate is unproductive, for all forms of evidence merit serious consideration. One important objective is to summarise 'facts' about economic time series which deserve further explanation. Viewed in conjunction with structural models, reduced forms may point to the importance of elements of the transmission mechanism not presently incorporated. In this sense, the two forms of evidence are complementary: reduced forms point to *whether* a variable is important, structural models to *how* it is important.

On this basis, reduced form studies in Britain for the 1960s cast doubt upon the view that 'money matters'. Single equation estimates of *money multipliers* which sought to explain movements in income directly from movements in monetary aggregates were generally unsuccessful (Artis and Nobay 1969, Goodhart and Crockett 1970). In order to determine why, Williams, Goodhart and Gowland (1976) investigated the causal relationship between money and income. They were unable to establish any clear-cut result which would point to the money supply being either demand-determined (as was assumed in studies of the demand for money) or exogenous to income (as assumed in the money multipliers). Causality tests with data for the 1970s, however, point to there having been a change in the pattern of causality with monetary aggregates having a greater causal role (Mills and Wood 1978, and Mills 1978b).

The main series under consideration are shown in figure 3.1. Fluctuations in Gross Domestic Product (GDP) at current market prices (compromise estimate) and prices (implicit GDP deflator) are dominated by three movements in the 1970s: acceleration in 1974—5, deceleration in 1976—7 and a resurgence of inflation in 1979 (which carried through 1980). If M1 is the preferred monetary aggregate then one must look to an approximately contemporaneous relationship between money and income (Savage 1980). This is difficult to interpret in terms of causation running from money to income unless the expectation of finding lags is ignored, although precedence in time is not necessarily an indicator of causality. In fact, Mills (1978b) finds evidence of causality running in the reverse direction from income to M1, a finding which is consistent with the treatment of M1 as demand-determined in demand for money functions. However, the behaviour of M1 in 1978 and 1979—80 is difficult to interpret in this vein, as we noted in Chapter 2.

If £M3 is the chosen aggregate, then a convincing correlation between money and incomes or prices necessitates assuming a substantial time lag — in the order of two years or more. A somewhat shorter, but still substantial, lag must be assumed

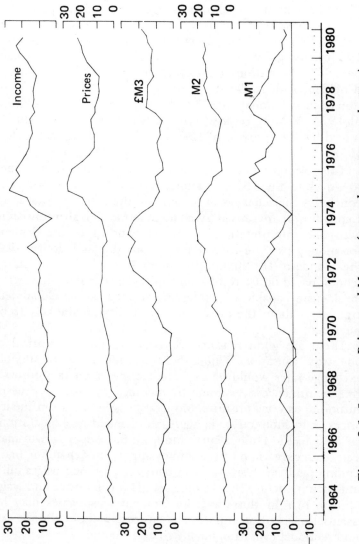

Figure 3.1 *Income, Prices and Money (annual percentage changes)*

if M2 (equal to M1 plus clearing bank time deposits)is the
indicator. Once this length of lag is accepted, then the association between monetary growth and price inflation is close.
Over the time period shown in figure 3.1, annual percentage
increases in £M3 (lagged two years) are able to account for
nearly 70% of annual percentage changes in GDP (Johnson
1980b). By allowing for longer lags, it is possible to 'explain'
over 90% of variations in the inflation rate by monetary growth
(Coghlan, 1980a). On these interpretations, the rapid expansion of broad money in 1972–3 is responsible for the inflation
of 1974–5. More recently, the 15% inflation rate in 1980 is
traced back to growth of £M3 of 15% and of M2 of 16.5% in
1978.

The notion of an exogenous influence running from money
to prices in the 1970s is supported by Mills (1978b), who
concludes that changes in income (in the form of Total Final
Expenditure) are caused by changes in M3. It is also consistent
with one interpretation of the breakdown of the demand
for money (see previous chapter). But the lag is longer than
the standard 18–20 months prediction of the monetarist
school, based on US results, and unless a plausible transmission
mechanism capable of explaining the lag can be elucidated,
arguments about the direction of causality are unlikely to be
silenced.

There are good reasons why one should be sceptical of
one way causation. While the transition to more flexible
exchange rates would be expected to give monetary forces a
greater influence over domestic incomes, the same is true of
autonomous wage pressure. Monetary developments influence
prices only indirectly, via aggregate demand or expectations
(at least in the Phillips curve models). But wages growth may
lead to an expansion of the money supply by expanding bank
lending (as firms borrow from banks to pay their wages bill),
and such monetary shocks may set off further price and wage
adjustments. In this way, the monetary aggregates may be
essential parts of an inflationary process without the idea of
unidirectional causation having to be accepted.

Transmission Mechanisms

Work on sketching out the transmission of money supply

disturbances in the UK, let alone the complex interactions above, is in its infancy, mainly because the econometric models have until recently been predicated on quite different assumptions. They have adopted an IS/LM type framework in which monetary policy begins with short term money market rates and proceeds to longer term yields and thence, in some cases via the stock market, to expenditures such as fixed investments. While the model-builders have worked assiduously to identify interest rate influences upon expenditures, the rewards have not been commensurate with effort (Savage 1978). Partly, this reflects the adequacy of measures of the expected rate of return on new investment and of the real cost of capital. With the latter, difficulties have been experienced in measuring the opportunity cost in ways which take account of inflation expectations and the different impact of inflation and taxation upon various areas of the corporate sector (see next chapter). It is also the case that policy sought to shield manufacturing industry as far as possible from interest rate variations, leaving the personal sector to bear the brunt. Thus the results are not indicative of the effect interest rates might have upon investment without this cosseting. Not surprisingly, the earlier versions of econometric models (such as those developed at the Treasury and the National Institute) based on the 1960s data sample find that monetary policy rested almost entirely on the impact of changes in hire purchase terms and the availability of bank lending upon personal consumption, and changes in the cost and availability of building society finance upon dwelling investment. In addition, alterations to domestic interest rates induced international capital flows, which the authorities could intervene to offset. These mechanisms still feature in these models, but the later versions (see Bladen-Hovell, Green and Savage 1981) incorporate, significantly, channels of monetary influence via wealth effects upon expenditures and via the exchange rate, to which we now turn.

Implicit in the interest rate mechanism is the assumption that equality between the demand and supply of money is maintained either by interest rate changes or by money stock changes when interest rates are policy-determined (but subject to variation). In either case it was supposed that the quantity of money supplied must be that demanded. If we accept, instead, that the quantity of money serves as a buffer stock, transactors can hold unwanted balances and be 'off' their demand curves. A money supply disturbance will initially be absorbed into portfolios and then partially removed through a variety of transactions some of which involve adjustments to the money stock and some of which alter the arguments of the demand function. Thus three channels exist for the resolution of 'monetary disequilibrium':

(i)   an interest rate effect bringing money demand temporarily or permanently into line with the new supply;
(ii) an expenditures effect, involving real income or prices, or which indirectly reduces the money supply (e.g. via tax payments or imports);
(iii) portfolio reallocations, like purchases of foreign or domestic assets, which alter either the money supply or the exchange rate (and hence either real income or prices).

Each corresponds to different views of the transmission mechanism: the first to the IS/LM system; the second to monetarism in a (partially) closed economy; the third to the monetary (or asset) theory of the balance of payments under either fixed or flexible exchange rates (for the latter, see articles contained in a special issue of *The Scandinavian Journal of Economics*, June 1976).

Notably, elements of the second and third mechanisms have begun to appear in econometric models of the UK economy, although only one model is structured explicitly around the 'monetary disequilibrium' idea (this is the 'small monetary model' developed at the Bank of England).[3] Because of the very general nature of the transmission mechanism implicit in this latter model, the empirical specification is largely *ad hoc* and the money stock £M3 itself (rather than monetary disequilibrium which ought to appear) is included in equations for expenditures (consumption and investment), prices and capital flows (with the latter influenced also by DCE). Thus in one way or another the model embraces all three channels above. With the second channel, other econometric models (e.g. the 'official' Bank of England model, 1979) include liquid assets (or liquid wealth) as a determinant of consumption expenditures. Liquid assets include building society and savings bank deposits. With the third channel, there have been a large number of attempts to model the impact of monetary aggregates upon exchange rates (in the London Business School, National Institute, Treasury and Bank of England models). Under the asset theory of exchange rates, the money supply may alter exchange rates either directly through purchases of foreign securities or indirectly as a determinant of expectations of exchange rate movements and thus of the yield of converting funds from one currency to another. Initial results for the UK appeared to indicate an important role for relative monetary growth rates in shaping exchange rate movements, but the equations have not proven to be as robust as was hoped.

These various channels could be circumvented, and the transmission of monetary policy speeded, if the money supply (or more generally, monetary policy) had a direct impact upon the employees' and companies' wage and price expectations. There is no firm evidence of this, partly because the announcement of monetary targets is a new avenue for policy, and also because expectations are unobservable. Various proxies suggest that, in the past, price expectations have been revised in the light of previous errors[4] in anticipations, augmented by a devaluation effect. Whilst the first suggests that monetary policy must affect prices before affecting expectations, the second suggests that transactors seek to anticipate factors relevant to price formation. It is this last mechanism, accompanied by the emphasis given in public discussion to monetary factors as a cause of inflation, which encourages the authorities to the belief that an impact via expectations can be counted on as an additional channel of monetary policy.

Nevertheless, it is fair to say that the transmission mechanism of monetary policy to ultimate goal variables remains shrouded in mystery. A variety of monetary aggregates (liquid assets, bank credit, DCE), not just £M3, seems relevant to expenditures, and aggregates other than £M3 could be used to influence expectations. Since the transmission seems likely to involve interest rate and exchange rate adjustments, these could feature as targets. This being the case, the choice of £M3 as the target must be further explained.

Exchange Rate Considerations

The choice of intermediate target is conditioned by the exchange rate regime. Where the authorities are required to defend a pegged exchange rate or give dominance to maintenance of a particular path of the exchange rate, the potential for achievement of a money supply target is limited by the scope for capital flows to eliminate international interest rate differentials. Intervention in the forward market allows some independence to be consistent with interest rate parity, by allowing the forward premium (as well as interest rates) to adjust to capital movements (Herring and Marston 1977). Exchange controls and the sterilisation of reserve flows by sales of public sector debt also give policy makers some breathing space. But the point remains that interest rate settings must take cognisance of external conditions and the money supply target is similarly constrained. Under these conditions, it is domestic credit and not the money supply over which the authorities have control, and this explains the IMF's wish for DCE targets to be set in line with nominal income goals to neutralise offsetting capital outflows.

Contrariwise, under a floating exchange rate, with external flows eliminated, the distinction between a DCE and money supply target evaporates. A money supply target is accordingly feasible, and the use of interest rates to control the money supply can also be contemplated. Of course, if real or nominal interest rates are out of line with those elsewhere, the capital flows so induced result in the authorities losing control of the exchange rate.

In practice, neither of these paradigms is an appropriate description of what has transpired since June 1972, when the exchange rate peg was lifted. At times the exchange rate has floated freely, at other times it has been more like a fixed rate, sometimes without official commitment but occasionally the intervention has been large. The intervention is on the grounds that temporary deviations of the actual from targeted monetary growth do not endanger longer run goals, because of the length of the time lags, whereas 'excessive' movements in the exchange rate rapidly feed through to imperil other objectives, such as international competitiveness or control of inflation. Some countries (Austria, Belgium and Sweden) have explicitly renounced monetary targets for an exchange rate commitment. In others (Switzerland and West Germany) experience demonstrates a considerable vulnerability of monetary targets to adverse exchange rate developments (excessive appreciations).

If the ties between exchange rate variations and consequent changes in prices and wages are close and the speed of transmission is fast, a policy of exchange rate targeting — that is, assigning the exchange rate to the prices objective by adopting a targeted rate of appreciation or depreciation — could be more effective as an anti-inflationary device than a monetary target. This is the question examined by Artis and Currie (1981). Employing an analysis reminiscent of that used by Poole (1970) for the choice between interest rates and the money supply, they compared the advantages of exchange rate versus monetary targets in achieving a price stability objective, but they were unable to come to any firm conclusion. It depends upon the nature of the shock, whether the source is foreign or domestic, the type of pricing behaviour adopted by firms, and on what evidence expectations of inflation are formed. As matters now stand these elements are necessarily judgmental, about which differences of view can reasonably be expected. In consequence, their results can be seen as a theoretical justification for intervention, an optimal strategy being for the authorities to alternate between a money supply and exchange rate target according to (their judgment about) the nature of the disturbance with which the economy is confronted at any time.

Why, then, has a money supply target alone been declared? Aside from simple failure to appreciate the full consequences of this choice, an important consideration in the authorities' thinking was no doubt the belief that flexibility can be mistaken for permissiveness, so that the whole intent of targets can be lost. The authorities feel that they must settle for *one* target if they are to establish credibility with the private sector and thereby gain a 'handle' upon expectations. A single, simple, monetary target leads itself to a neat medium-term prescription in a way that a more complicated rule could not do. Moreover, the most recent experience of exchange rate support may have unnerved them. In the environment of the 1980s, in which internationally short term capital is highly mobile, an exchange rate target out of line with the market's perceptions is not easily sustained. For example, the authorities 'capped' the exchange rate against upward pressures between January and October 1977 and took in $11 billion of net reserve inflows. An exchange rate target is, therefore, a less effective discipline over the consequences of 'excessive' domestic credit expansion arising from bank lending and fiscal deficits. (Here in describing the authorities' thinking we must dissent and record that neither bank lending nor fiscal deficits need necessarily imply monetary creation. It depends upon the course of interest rates.) If so, why is the target not set in terms of DCE?

DCE versus Money

Targets for DCE co-existed with targets for broad money until the beginning of 1979. Since then, the authorities have set targets for £M3 alone. As is apparent from table 3.1 (page 40), these latter targets have been attained with domestic credit creation in excess of the increases in the money supply, £M3. Coghlan (1980b) argues that the current account deficit in 1979, despite North Sea oil exports, can be attributed to the external leakage of money occasioned by excessive DCE.

Most of the interest in DCE is as a target supplementary to £M3. The reason why DCE may not be an adequate sole indicator is its weaker capacity to explain the behaviour of output and prices. There is also the belief that expectations of future inflation rates and exchange rates depend primarily on money supply behaviour, because of the appeal of simple monetarism as formulated in the relatively closed economy conditions of the United States. On the other hand, the strength of DCE lies in its capacity to indicate potential external imbalances, given information on the demand for money, when the authorities are intervening in the exchange market.

Broadly speaking, the increase in £M3 equals DCE plus reserve flows (but see the next chapter for some important qualifications). The £M3 target could be met with a high DCE and a heavy private sector outflow of funds abroad. In the longer run this position could not be sustained, as the home country would run out of reserves or the exchange rate would fall. What the addition of a DCE target does is to ensure that a £M3 target achieved at the cost of a large unanticipated external outflow is an unacceptable result in the short run as well.

At issue here is the degree of discretion which it is desirable to leave in the hands of the authorities. They undoubtedly agree also that the situation described above is untenable, for they monitor both groups of liabilities making up £M3. Use of more than one target, as opposed to indicator, could be said to over-constrain the system, and result in conflicting signals for policy. Further, as the Governor noted in 1978, the public impact of the exercise of setting targets, if that is considered worth preserving, might be reduced in the process. (Interestingly, in the USA where there are multiple targets, public discussion has tended to focus on one of the three targets). Finally, the advantage of a DCE target comes from its use in conjunction with a broad money target. It does seem strange to use as a target an aggregate for which there is no evidence (other than that reported in Chapter 2) of a stable demand function, whereas a stable function has been identified for M1.

Narrow Money

In fact, the case for M1 as a target rests almost entirely, and in our view incorrectly, around the evidence pointing to a stable demand function. This may seem paradoxical, but on our interpretation the fact that a short run demand function for M1 in *nominal* terms can be identified with fair success means that the stock must to a large extent be demand-determined. If this is the case, the aggregate may be controllable via demand, but if the arguments (the price level and real expenditures) are the goal variables, they cannot necessarily be influenced by M1 — in fact the function says the reverse is the case. That is, an equation in which M1 is demand-determined is no evidence of how the demand function would behave if causation were reversed. For the same reason, the evidence given earlier in this chapter may not be relevant for assessing the likely impact of using M1 as a control variable.

It must be asked how M1 would serve as a control variable. Higher interest rates, say, may merely lead bank depositors to shift funds out of current accounts into time or savings deposit with banks, without altering the total. Because of these substitutions the demand for M1 may be highly elastic with respect to interest rates, so that small variations in rates enable an M1 target to be satisfied, but what if anything has been altered along the way?

A somewhat different case can, however, be made out for an M1 target. It is based on three propositions: (a) interest rates are the vehicle by which monetary policy is transmitted to expenditures; (b) a money supply target is needed for identification with the public; (c) M1 is sensitive, but not unduly so, to interest rates. In these circumstances M1 could serve as a cosmetic indicator of policy. That is, interest rates would do the work in terms of restraining output and prices, with M1 providing an indication of the restriction of transaction balances, without itself contributing to the process except via public perceptions. In this way, the money supply target would be readily achieved, but it would be partly a charade. M1 balances would still be shifted into time deposits when interest rates rise and while this is largely if not entirely cosmetic, it both allows time for interest rates to work through to the real economy and convinces the public that appropriate action has been taken.

This is a not implausible scenario of how money supply targets probably work in countries with M1 targets, but it can be queried on several grounds. First, the idea that interest rates are the chief transmitter ignores the 'monetary disequilibrium' mechanism. Second, to control M1, the authorities must be able to vary the gap between the own rate on M1 and that on short term paper. Maintenance of this relationship requires continuity of the institutional arrangements which make the return on current accounts sticky. Third, the value of a money supply target over an interest rate target in such circumstances seems questionable.

Which Broad Money Aggregate?

A broad money target has been chosen in preference to M1 because alterations are required to the banking sector's total balance sheet in order to effect changes in broad money, and these alterations are thought to have greater significance for developments in the economy. But which of the broad aggregates is appropriate?

Table 3.2 sets out annual growth rates of some of the aggregates which are, or are soon to be, monitored in the Bank (DCE has been omitted). M3 and £M3 have featured as indicators for many years. PSL1 and PSL2, the liquidity aggregates, are now closely watched in the Bank. They first appeared in the Bank's Quarterly Bulletin in September 1979, but have been largely ignored by outside commentators. M2

Table 3.2 Growth Rates of Various Monetary Aggregates

	M1	M2A	M2	£M3	M3	PSL1	PSL2
1972	14.2	10.2	17.0	26.5	27.8		
1973	5.1	10.4	21.6	26.0	27.6		
1974	10.8	17.5	19.3	10.2	12.6		
1975	18.6	11.8	6.2	6.5	7.6		
1976	11.4	7.0	8.9	9.5	11.2	8.7	10.4
1977	21.5	12.8	8.9	10.0	9.8	8.2	11.6
1978	16.4	14.0	16.4	15.0	14.9	15.6	15.0
1979	9.1	15.8	16.9	12.6	12.3	16.8	13.7
1980	3.9	n.a.	n.a.	18.6	18.5	16.0	14.1

Definitions:

M1 = Currency *plus* private sector sterling sight deposits.

M2A = M1 *plus* 'retail' time deposits at Deposit Banks and Discount Houses.

M2 = M2A *plus* 'wholesale' time deposits at Deposit Banks.

£M3 = M2 *plus* time deposits at other banks, public sector deposits and sterling CDs

M3 = £M3 *plus* deposits in other currencies.

PSL1 = Private sector holdings of £M3 *plus* money market instruments (bills, deposits with Local Authorities and Finance Houses) *plus* Certificates of Tax Deposits.

PSL2 = PSL1 *plus* Building Society and other savings deposits.

and M2A are our estimates of the old M2 definition, based around clearing banks' deposits. More refined data are now being collected by the Bank to put these estimates on a firmer statistical basis.

Why has £M3 been chosen as the monetary target in preference to one of the other aggregates? Obviously data considerations have militated against the liquidity and M2 aggregates, for there is insufficient experience yet of their behaviour and association with goal variables. In the case of M2A, its collection is designed around a possible switch to monetary base control which we consider in Chapter 6. But there are other reasons.

M3 used to be the target. It differs from £M3 by reason of deposits held by UK residents with UK banks in non-sterling (i.e., other) currencies. A survey in 1976 of the holders of these foreign currency balances showed that they were primarily UK firms (notably oil and insurance companies) with continuing business abroad and that the balances held related primarily to the level of overseas business. It seemed unlikely that the balances played much part in their UK business. On such grounds the focus switched to £M3. This use of the belances included in M3 but not in £M3 was in large part a consequence of the exchange controls then in force. With the abolition of controls, UK residents are able to diversify their money holdings into different currencies. M3 may then become of greater significance. Sterling deposits and foreign currency deposits held with banks abroad (i.e. in Euromarkets) may also assume greater importance. These issues are taken up in Chapter 7.

One point in favour of £M3 over some of the other aggregates is that it has been possible for it to be related, through balance sheet identities, to other important magnitudes. In particular, the growth in £M3 can be analysed in terms of its credit counterparts, comprising the public sector borrowing requirement (PSBR), public sector debt sales to non-banks, external flows, and all banks' lending to the private sector. By equating these with respectively fiscal policy, debt management (and monetary) policy, exchange rate policy and banking policy, developments in £M3 show in a clear statistical format the separate and combined influence of a range of policies. Analysis in this format has served as a 'consistency test' of the various fields of policy with monetary control objectives, and as a way of constraining politicians in terms of public spending. This way of examining the money supply is analysed in Chapter 4. Meanwhile, we note that by redefining 'bank lending' appropriately, the framework could be made consistent with definitions of money embracing particular categories of bank (e.g. M2) or broader groupings of institutions (e.g. building societies, savings banks). But it is not possible to do so for M1, since the division of liabilities into time or sight deposits cannot be readily predicted in the framework.

As an indicator, £M3 lies about halfway along the liquidity scale. It is less controllable than M1, but may be more so than, say, PSL2. Because of its position, it may be seen as a good (the best?) compromise indicator of how the financial system is responding to monetary policy and transmitting it to the goal variables. This is an empirical question of how the various components of liquidity respond to monetary policy, which we take up in Chapters 5 and 6. We may also note that in the last few years, £M3 has not been a good guide to the behaviour of other aggregates. In 1978 and 1979, M2 and the PSL indicators grew at a significantly faster rate than £M3. In 1980, £M3 expanded more rapidly than the PSL measures. This behaviour has been attributed in policy circles to distortions introduced by the monetary controls used prior to the 1980 reforms, but other factors may be at work, which we also examine later. For the moment we stay with £M3 as the target in order to describe the workings of present control procedures.

Notes to Chapter 3

1. The theoretical rationale for this argument comes from the monetary theory of the balance of payments. See H.G. Johnson (1972).
2. Friedman (1977) advanced the idea of a medium run positive relationship between inflation and unemployment which is additional to the short run inverse relationship. If we add a long run vertical relationship when all uncertainties and expectations are washed out, there are in effect three Phillips curves. The similarity of British Conservative government views about these relationships with earlier Australian government views is examined in Lewis (1981).

3. See Coghlan (1979), Hilliard (1980) and Hoffman (1980). A disequilibrium model has been developed at the Reserve Bank of Australia, see Jonson, Moses and Wymer (1977).

4. This error learning process explains why the authorities have preferred a 'gradualist' monetary strategy, in contradistinction to some rational expectations models which imply that inflation can be stopped in its tracks by stopping monetary growth, without massive unemployment.

4

Controlling the Supply of Money

For reasons spelt out in the previous chapter, achievement of a money supply target is central to present monetary policy (indeed, of policy since 1974). When the money supply is forecast to grow at a rate inconsistent with the target, interest rates are being changed to bring it back within target. The basic premise is that higher interest rates restrain monetary growth.

It is tempting to suppose then, that monetary control is achieved by 'sliding up and down' the demand for money schedule, to use Parkin's (1978) terminology. However, this picture is rather misleading; in the short run, the demand for £M3, the chosen aggregate, depends on the differential between market rates and bank deposit rates, and this is not a margin which responds readily or reliably to policy actions. Rather, the authorities operate on the 'supply side' counterparts of £M3 — the PSBR, sales of public sector debt, reserve flows and bank lending to the private sector. When interest rates are changed it is with the objective of altering one or more of these components.

Whether this can be held to avoid the problem posed by competitive bank deposit rates depends on how we interpret the result. On the view favoured by the Treasury and some other model-builders (National Institute, London Business School), the financial sector is appropriately treated as an equilibrium system, so that the stock of money is always at a level consistent with the public's demand. Although the stock of money is determined residually, as a consequence of the interaction of external flows, government spending, tax policies and credit market developments, the stock so supplied is assumed to be always willingly held. Thus the balance sheet identities imply a demand for money function, overall equality between the demand and supply of financial assets giving money market equilibrium. Policy is still, by implication, operating upon demand, even though the function is not explicitly estimated.

This interpretation needs to be distinguished from the alternative 'disequilibrium' approach, discussed in earlier chapters and favoured in some quarters of the Bank of England. Here the possibility arises of shifting the supply schedule of money independently of (or reinforcing) any influence of policy upon demand. In turn, the unanticipated difference between the demand and supply of money carries implications for, and exerts an independent influence upon, asset and goods markets. Policy still relies upon there being long run stability of the demand for money, but because supply shocks are not immediately and entirely accommodated by changes in demand, it is no longer necessary to establish this stability on a quarter-by-quarter basis. The approach thus offers ready explanation for the inability to identify a short run demand function for £M3.

Whatever is the correct rationale, the approach justifies the authorities' preference for £M3 over M1. The major ways of inducing supply side shifts revolve around the aggregate balance sheet of the banking system. Policy can be thought of as proceeding to the monetary target in two stages: first, the use of policy instruments to alter the structure of interest rates; second, the influence of interest rates upon the supply side components of £M3.

Controls Over Interest Rates

Transactions in government securities are the centrepiece. Open market operations are not concentrated in the gilt-edged market, but in the discount market, with the aim of influencing short term interest rates and thus encouraging changes across the whole structure of rates. This is not to say that the authorities do not influence long term rates directly; indeed, given the size of the funding programme, they could not help but do so. (The ratio of government stock outstanding to GDP is probably higher in Britain than in any other country — see Tew 1978). For reasons examined below, the authorities exercise considerable restraint in the conduct of open market operations in long term debt. Accordingly, this influence ranks as a somewhat constrained policy weapon alongside operations in short term debt.

In 1971, it was envisaged that control over interest rates could be exercised additionally via the liquidity of the banking system. This 'second leg' of interest rate policy required the banks to sell off investments as calls to Special Deposits interacted against the 12.5% reserve asset ratio. As the conversion of the reserve assets ratio from a monetary instrument to a prudential control indicates, this system has not worked as intended. The reason is not just, as argued by the authorities, the practice of 'liability management' by the banks, whereby the banks bid for deposits rather than sell off investments when short of reserves. Banks have been provided with an incentive to bid for reserves rather than manage assets because reserve assets have been capable of being generated fairly freely by the banking system. But unlike in Australia, from where the reserve assets system was borrowed, the target was not to alter banks' credit creation.[1] Instead, the target was interest rates (an intention which was overlooked in the academic literature). For this reason, the authorities have not been as worried as outside commentators by the fact that the supply of reserve assets has not been totally under the control of the Bank. Interest rates could still be influenced via the discount market.

Thus the traditional tools of Bank rate (known since 1972 as Minimum Lending Rate, MLR) and the bill tender remain the major instruments. Since May 1978, MLR has been administered by the Bank and has relevance in two ways. Announcements of the level of MLR have a significant impact upon market expectations of the appropriate level of short term rates. Second, and underlying the first effect, the authorities can always ensure that the discount houses are short of cash. Only the discount houses have access to lender of last resort facilities at the Bank, and they act as intermediary between the Bank and the banking system. Their shortage of cash is relieved by lending at MLR, which is generally above the return on the houses' asset portfolio, so encouraging higher interest rates on their new borrowings and in the market generally. Because the market knows that changes in MLR are made effective in this manner, MLR serves as a signal for other rates to alter — rates on short term deposits with local authorities and finance houses, and bank overdrafts.

Suppose that the authorities wish to counteract a downward pressure on interest rates. It is customary for them always to issue a few more bills than they predict that the market will have the funds to take up in the coming week — in effect there is a deliberate overissue of bills. Because the discount houses are obliged, by long-standing agreement with the Bank, to contract to buy up ('cover the tender' for) all bills offered for sale, this has an effect equivalent to the Bank selling the bills in the open market. The consequent shortage of cash forces the discount market 'into Bank' to borrow at MLR for seven days. If the market is held taut in this way, it allows the authorities to relieve the tension at the interest rate structure of their choice, so influencing the course of other short term rates.

In order to create a shortage of cash, the Bank must know the banking system's cash position, for this determines whether the banks are in a position to lend to the market. Essentially, the discount markets' cash requirement is a reflection of the banks' cash position ('cash' being currency plus balances with the Bank of England). Only the clearing banks use balances with the Bank as working balances, and since 1971 they have had to maintain 1.5% of their eligible liabilities in this form (before 1971 they maintained an 8% cash ratio). This ratio (like the old cash ratio) has not been used as a means of controlling bank deposits via a 'money multiplier', and the clearers do not have to meet the requirement on any particular day or over any exactly specified period. Rather, the ratio is used informally as an aid to predicting by how much Treasury bills need to be overissued to engineer a shortage of cash, which shortage is then supplied back to the system at a price consistent with the desired interest rate structure.

Neither the mandatory cash ratio nor the discount houses' agreement to underwrite the weekly Treasury bill tender are really necessary; both are a reflection of the Bank's willingness to provide cash. This was made clear when the then Chief Cashier appeared before the Radcliffe Committee in 1957. Under questioning, he revealed that the discount market would not be prepared to cover the tender without the assurance that the necessary cash would be made available.[2] Thus it is the Bank which covers the tender. These arrangements, peculiar to the UK, may not have made the system materially different from that in other countries in the final result, but there has been a distortion of the intention of last resort loans. Support by the Bank to keep the clearing banks above their 1.5% ratio has been very frequent — almost daily — some in the form of loans at MLR, other by the discounting of bills at ongoing market rates (Congdon 1980c). To use Brian Griffiths' (1980) evocative phrase, last resort loans have been made into 'first resort loans'.

As part of the 1980 reforms, the tactics outlined above are beginning to undergo change. Future operations upon short term rates will still be conducted in the bill markets (although the possibility of operations in the interbank market was considered), and will still be with the discount houses.[3] However, the technique of creating an initial shortage of cash and then subsequently providing it again via the discount window is being phased out.

> The changes in the Bank's methods of operation . . . are designed to allow the authorities to put greater emphasis on open market operations than on discount window lending when relieving cash shortages . . .
>
> Changes in this respect had begun as early as August [1980] . . . to encourage discount houses to sell bills to the Bank in circumstances when previously they might have preferred to borrow from the bank.
>
> *BEQB*, March 1981, p. 24

This in itself changes nothing, but the clear intention is for short term interest rates to be set more by market forces and less by the Bank. Rather than aim for a particular *rate* consistent with its monetary objectives, the operational target is now to be one of keeping short term rates (including MLR) within an unpublished *band*. (Tew (1981) provides an alternative account of the new proposals.)

If the market is not longer sure at what price cash is to be provided, the possibility is also open for the Bank to move towards monetary base control.

> While no decision has been taken to introduce monetary base control, which would represent an important change of policy, the present moves would be consistent with a gradual evolution in that direction.
> *BEQB*, March 1981, p. 21

At present, cash is squeezed but only to the extent necessary to enforce a particular level (or band) of interest rates. Under monetary base control, the squeeze would be continued until banks' balance sheets came into line. This is explained in Chapter 6. For the moment we stay with the present system and examine the impact of interest rates upon the money supply via the 'supply side' components.

Factors Affecting the Money Supply

The money supply, £M3, consists of

£M3 = Notes and coin held by the public
+ Sterling deposits of UK public and private sectors (i.e. UK residents).

These bank deposits are one item of the UK banking sector's balance sheet. This is as follows:

UK Banks' Balance Sheet

Liabilities	Assets
Sterling deposits of UK residents	Sterling lending to UK public sector
Sterling deposits of overseas residents	Sterling lending to UK private sector
Non-deposit liabilities	Sterling lending to overseas residents
Foreign currency deposits	Foreign currency assets

From the balance sheet it is apparent that not all increases in lending in sterling by the banks need be matched by increases in sterling deposits held by UK residents and thus enter into £M3. In particular, there may be increases in non-deposit liabilities. Increases in these liabilities represent additions to capital reserves and internal funds net of additions to non-financial assets (land, buildings etc). Second, overseas residents are also holders of sterling deposits. A use of these deposits for sterling lending is excluded from the money supply statistics. Third, UK banks accept deposits in foreign currencies and make loans in foreign currencies to both residents and non-residents. A switch from foreign currency assets into sterling assets ('switching in') allows banks to increase their sterling lending, again without expanding the money supply. These three ways by which the growth in the money supply may differ from the growth of bank lending become clear when the balance sheet identity is used to express increases in sterling deposits of UK residents as the change in all the rest, with appropriate signs.

Increase in £M3 equals:

Increase in: Notes and coin held by the public
                    Sterling lending to UK public sector
                    Sterling lending to UK private sector
                    Sterling lending to overseas residents

minus increase in: Overseas sterling deposits
                    Foreign currency deposits net of f.c. assets
                    Non-deposit liabilities

The extent of bank lending to the public sector reflects the balance of government transactions with the private sector and overseas sector. An excess of government expenditure over receipts, termed the public sector borrowing requirement (PSBR), can be financed in four ways: (i) by issue of notes and coin to the public; (ii) by issue of bonds to the public; (iii) by finance accruing from overseas (including a fall in official reserves); (iv) by borrowing from the banking system. That is,

PSBR equals: Increase in the notes and coin held by the public
+ Sales of public sector debt to UK private non-bank sector
+ External finance of public sector
+ Increase in sterling lending to public sector.

It is now possible to replace the item 'increase in sterling lending to the public sector' with the PSBR and the other items (entered with appropriate signs), in which case the two entries for notes and coin cancel out:

Increase in £M3 equals:

   PSBR
— Sales of public sector debt to UK private non-bank sector
+ Increase in sterling lending to UK private sector
+ Increase in sterling lending to overseas residents
— External finance of public sector
— Increase in overseas sterling deposits
— Increase in foreign currency deposits net of f.c. assets
— Increase in non-deposit liabilities of banks

In shorthand notation:

   PSBR
— Gilt sales
+ Increase in bank lending
equals DCE
+ Net external flows
— Increase in non-deposit liabilities
equals Increase in £M3

This simple framework, based on the balance sheet identities of the banking system and government financing, now forms the basis of monetary control, and of public discussion of it, in Britain. Because DCE relates to the asset, or lending side, of banks' balance sheet, the Bank is able to satisfy those who argue that bank credit and not the money supply should be the focus of policy, since the target subsumes it. Moreover, because the PSBR, gilt sales and external flows can be identified with fiscal policy, debt management, and exchange rate

Table 4.1 Sources of Money Supply Growth, 1963–79, £m

	PSBR	Gilt Sales	Increase in Bank Lending	Net External Flows	Increase in Non-deposit Liabilities	Increase in £M3
Average 1963–71	892	−562	825	46	−113	1,087
1972	2,034	−1,006	5,646	−1,095	−625	4,927
1973	4,195	−2,292	6,161	−877	−485	6,702
1974	6,387	−3,177	3,724	−2,997	−682	3,255
1975	10,494	−5,560	−405	−1,300	−898	2,331
1976	9,152	−5,800	4,115	−2,723	−1,179	3,565
1977	5,955	−8,464	3,593	+3,448	−400	4,132
1978	8,350	−6,043	5,760	−380	−915	6,772
1979	12,620	−10,869	8,574	−2,892	−818	6,615
1980	12,463	−9,729	12,822	−3,321	−1,338	10,897

policies respectively, the framework shows the interrelation-
ship of the various arms of economic policy.

Table 4.1 shows the contribution of each of the five
groupings of components distinguished above to the growth
of the money supply since 1963. The approach presently
followed by the authorities begins with a forecast of each of
these components at existing interest rates (and other policy
settings). For all practical purposes attention can be focused
upon four: the growth of non-deposit liabilities picks up
errors in the accounting system, but its longer run path
reflects the banks' own capital funds and reserves, items
which have proven to be more predictable than the others. If
the forecast of the items taken together implies that the
money supply is growing at a rate, say, in excess of that
targeted for, there is the expectation that one or more of the
four components will respond to higher interest rates so as to
restrict the rate of monetary growth.

The other arms of policy are also available, but they are
tied to other objectives and the extent to which they can be
co-opted for monetary control depends on the time horizon
of the control problem. Some of the conflicts between
exchange rate management and monetary control have eventually been resolved by allowing exchange rates to change (as
in 1977). The longer run path of fiscal policy is, since 1979,
being planned with monetary objectives in mind. But interest
rates remain the major short to medium run control. The
contribution of the other policies depends upon the source of
the monetary disturbance and is best discussed under the
various headings.

External Influences

From the viewpoint of monetary controls, external flows
might be expected to respond perversely to interest rates, as
private capital flows in across the exchanges, expanding international reserves and the money supply. But the external
influences upon the money supply embrace much more than
the movement in international reserves. Accordingly the
widely used identity relating the change in money supply to

DCE plus the change in reserves (which in turn can be related to the current and capital account of the balance of payments) is no more than a first approximation. How much of an approximation it is can be indicated by noting that

$$\Delta \pounds M3 = DCE + \text{changes in reserves}$$
$$- \Delta(\text{government borrowing from overseas})$$
$$- \Delta(\text{overseas } \pounds \text{ deposits})$$
$$- \Delta(\text{switched position})$$
$$- \Delta(\text{non-deposit liabilities}).$$

Non-deposit liabilities have already been discussed. Our analysis of the other items is based on Goodhart (1978). *Government borrowing from overseas* occurs when an overseas resident purchases sterling from the authorities and uses that to invest in UK public sector debt, such as gilts or Treasury bills. As a result of the transaction, official liabilities to and assets of non-residents are written up by an equal amount without affecting DCE or M3. In the case of the other items, DCE may rise (as if there is an increase in bank lending) but since residents' sterling deposits are unaffected, there is also no increase in £M3. *Overseas sterling deposits* are excluded from the money supply because they are considered to consist largely of 'speculative' balances, with little immediate influence upon domestic expenditure decisions. Banks' *switch* into sterling when they issue foreign currency deposits in order to acquire sterling assets. Switching-in can be on a covered basis, by means of a swap transaction, whereby a spot sale of foreign currency in order to purchase sterling is covered by a forward re-purchase of the same foreign currency for delivery at a later date against domestic currency. Alternatively, the switch may be uncovered, in which case the bank is taking a position in foreign currency for investment reasons (a 'short' position). Prudential considerations (previously exchange control regulations), limit banks' uncovered position. In both cases, the sterling funds so created are subject to reserve requirements.

These three items may be expected to reflect international interest rate differentials (covered and uncovered) and exchange rate expectations. Table 4.2 shows their movement in recent years. A comparison of 1976 (when sterling was weak)

Table 4.2 External Components of Money Supply Growth

	1976	1977	1978	1979	1980
Increase in £M3, £m	3,565	4,132	6,772	6,615	10,897
of which					
DCE	7,467	1,084	8,067	10,325	15,556
Official Financing	−3,629	+7,604	−1,504	1,445	880
Other Public Sector External Financing	+624	−2,113	+537	−871	−935
Overseas £ Deposits (− increase)	−142	−1,639	−36	−2,999	−3,003
Banks' Foreign Currency Deposits Net of f.c. Assets (− increase)	+424	−404	+623	−467	−263
Non-deposit Liabilities (− increase)	−1,179	−400	−915	−818	−1,338

with 1977 (when sterling was strong) shows that as the pound strengthened, foreigners acquired sterling securities and bank deposits, while banks moved to a switched-in position. In 1977, the authorities resisted the rise in the value of the pound because of worries about the competitiveness of manufacturing, and international reserves (i.e. official financing of the balance of payments) increased. Because a sizeable proportion of that increase finished up in non-residents' hands, reserve flows greatly exceeded net external influences upon the money supply.

In 1979 and also in 1980, sterling was also strong. Yet because of the greater flexibility of the exchange rate (an appreciation was seen as desirable to keep down domestic prices of imported goods) reserve flows contributed little to overall monetary growth. Indeed, net external flows acted to reduce the money supply as banks expanded their lending by inducing overseas residents to hold sterling deposits and by switching foreign currency deposits into sterling lending. The strength of the pound, high nominal interest rates and (until mid-1980) a desire by banks to avoid the penalties of the 'corset'[4] all provided incentives for banks and foreigners to undertake the transactions.

In Chapter 3, we noted that the reliability of £M3 as an indicator of the behaviour of the broad monetary aggregates has been questioned, because the other aggregates grew more rapidly than £M3 in 1978 and 1979 when the authorities sought to restrain monetary growth. In 1979, £M3 also underestimated the growth of the 'credit' counterparts in the economy, with DCE far in excess of the increase in £M3. As we have seen, it was the banking sector (and not the public sector) which contributed to this result. A pecularity of Special Deposits (and the old reserve asset ratio and the 'corset') is that they are (were) applied to eligible liabilities (ELs), not to the deposit component of £M3. The two differ in several ways, but a major difference is the inclusion of overseas £ deposits in ELs but not in £M3. Johnson (1980a) argued for the redefinition of £M3 (or of the monetary target) to include these deposits, which would serve to bring £M3, ELs and DCE closer together.

The problem here is that a freely floating exchange rate, which succeeds in reducing to zero the official financing of the balance of payments, isolates the money supply from reserve flows, but does not reduce to zero the influence of net external flows upon the money supply. A surplus in the balance of payments (current plus capital account) can be financed by foreigners drawing down accumulated £ deposits. On one view, net external effects can be shut off only when the exchange rate is driven to a level where the balance of payments surplus becomes zero. In the absence of this degree of exchange rate flexibility, the authorities may look to other controls over movements in overseas £ deposits (e.g. exchange controls or some form of tax). In March 1981, the authorities introduced provisions for levying an interest rate tax upon overseas £ deposits and for controlling sales of money market paper to foreigners, for use in the event of sudden pressure on the exchange rate. (Controls were also introduced for possible application to residents' overseas borrowing — thus covering another source of capital flow).

PSBR and Gilt Sales

In the Green Paper on monetary control, the main monetary instruments are described as being 'fiscal policy and interest rates': the former being taxation and expenditure policies to alter the PSBR, the latter to influence, amongst other things, sales of public sector debt. In line with its 'medium run' monetary objectives, announced in April 1980, the government is aiming to bring the PSBR as a proportion of national income down over time. This citing of fiscal policy as a monetary instrument came under attack by economists in later submissions to the House of Commons Civil Service Committee. Interestingly, perhaps the most trenchant criticism of this view came from Milton Friedman (1980b) and not from some of the Keynesians.

Friedman said that there was no necessary connection between the government budget and the quantity of money. The present relationship between the two came about, he said, only because of the undesirable techniques which the British authorities use to control the supply of money. Friedman's alternative is considered in Chapter 6. For the present we note that despite the attention which has been given to the PSBR as a source of monetary expansion, there is only a weak relationship between the two. An inspection of table 4.1 indicates, if anything, an inverse relationship between the PSBR and changes in £M3, which is confirmed by regression analysis (Savage 1980).

It is always open for the authorities to undertake trans-actions in public sector debt and, if necessary, alter interest rates so as to make the government deficit consistent with the monetary target. In recent years the PSBR has been large, but sales of gilts and other public debt to the non-bank private sector have meant that very little finance has been provided by the banking system. Nevertheless, the authorities argue that a heavy burden has been imposed on techniques of debt management leaving them persistently vulnerable to the moods of the gilt-edged market. A reduction in the PSBR by fiscal policy would, they argue, enable the monetary target to be met at a lower level of interest rates, thereby 'crowding out' less private expenditures. Without this reduction in public sector borrowings, interest rates are 'too high'.

There are several difficulties with this line of reasoning. First, the PSBR is not a policy variable. With given tax scales and expenditure programmes, its size will vary with the level of activity and prices, as taxation receipts and social welfare

spending change. A policy of fiscal restraint (cutting government spending programmes and raising tax rates) may not
succeed in reducing the PSBR to the desired extent, if in the
process economic activity falls off and unemployment is
increased. This reduction in income may in turn serve to
reduce the money supply, either through the reduced demand
for money or for bank advances, but it is an indirect method
of controlling the money supply. Second, interest rates may
not be reduced merely by lowering the PSBR. There is not a
fixed pool of loanable funds. A smaller PSBR reduces the
demand for funds for government financing but if income is
depressed, then savings and profits and so the supply of
loanable funds may also be less (Hahn 1980). Any tendency
for (real) interest rates to fall comes from a 'dishoarding' of
money via a reduced transactions demand for money, not
from the PSBR.

This last point can usefully be reversed to explain why
interest rates tend to increase when the PSBR increases.
Interest rates will increase if the fiscal changes succeed in
raising output and incomes, and hence the demand for money.
But if income is unchanged, interest rates may not change
even if gilts are sold to maintain the monetary target. The gilts
and other public sector debt which are sold to finance the
PSBR merely mop up liquidity previously injected into the
economy from the government spending in excess of tax
receipts. That is, it is the income expansion and not the
PSBR itself which is responsible for interest rates rising. This
discussion ignores the wealth constraint on the demand for
money and the need for 'portfolio balance' between money,
bonds and capital. On these grounds it may be argued that
interest rates have to rise to induce wealth holders to hold
more bonds even if income does not increase. But for this
comparison it is the *real* value of government indebtedness,
and increases in it, which are important. The major consequences for interest rates come from the real PSBR not the
nominal PSBR, a distinction which Taylor and Threadgold's
(1979) analysis has highlighted.

A discussion of the debt management implications of the
PSBR cannot be divorced from present techniques in the gilt-
edged market. Considerations of monetary control have, in

the past, been subordinated to the objective of assisting the government to borrow on the most advantageous terms. Britain has an unusually large national debt so that the PSBR is augmented by maturities which require re-financing. Also unusual is the extent of long-dated maturities whose value is sensitive to yield variations. An orderly market, with steady gilt prices, has been sought to maximise official sales of bonds in the longer run.

Despite significant revisions to operating strategies in recent years (described in the *Bank of England Quarterly Bulletin*, June 1979), traditional attitudes persist, and the Bank feels constrained in undertaking open market operations with a direct quantity objective. Instead, the Bank uses its influence over short term rates to encourage changes at the long end and induce demand for gilts. Under the so-called 'cashier's theory', this demand is a negative function of the change in interest rates, as well as a positive function of the level of rates. Gilts can be sold when interest rates are expected to fall, but considerable restraint must be exercised in contemplating sales when interest rates are expected either to rise or to rise further following an initial upward movement. Hence the so-called 'Grand Old Duke of York' tactics. A sharp and large upward shift in short rates is engineered. This is to generate expectations that rates will later fall and that there are capital gains to be had from immediate purchases. After the sales, there follows a slower decline in rates.

These tactics can produce large sales of gilts, but the sales are variable and difficult to predict. This, and the feeling that the interest rate changes may destabilise the real economy, have prompted an examination of alternatives. One is a broader market in short term securities (*BEQB*, December 1980, p. 429). Gilts may be difficult to sell when extrapolative expectations take hold, but the cashier's theory does not explain why short term paper, less subject to changes in capital value, cannot be sold in these circumstances. One inhibiting factor has been the reserve assets ratio. As banks have endeavoured to 'sell' deposits and buy reserves to sustain their lending, yields on reserve assets, especially Treasury bills, have declined relative to those on bank deposits. In the process, they become less attractive than bank deposits to the non-bank public. Now that the reserve assets ratio has been dropped as a monetary control, there is the opportunity to explore a broader non-bank market in short term public sector securities.

Any shortening of the maturities of public sector debt, given the size of outstanding stocks, has implications for future funding operations. Until now, the authorities have deliberately sought a long average maturity so as to maintain control over the liquidity flow between the public and private sectors. An issue of more short term securities could alter this.

> If you [say] halved the average maturity, you would in turn, by and large, double the flow of maturities to be financed each year. Far from holding the market taut, it gives the central banker a feeling of rushing around with a mop trying to sop up floods of liquidity. This is not a comfortable posture. Instead of us feeling that we are in charge, able to relieve the market on our own terms, we are left with the feeling that our ability to control either monetary aggregates, or interest rates, or a preferred trade-off between these objectives is weakened and made far less predictable by an overhang of short term debt.
>
> Goodhart (1973)

Enough other central bankers have echoed this view to suggest that there might be a gap between actual experience and economic analysis of it. Outside economists are generally sceptical of the problems posed by funding, arguing on the basis of liquidity preference theory that the demand for government securities at a particular structure of interest rates is a desire for an outstanding stock. If interest rates are attractive, redemptions should be replaced by new issues within the stock demand. It is not altogether clear that the same time sequence of interest rate implications always follows from a loanable funds model of interest rate determination, and this is one area which might merit further investigation.

Amongst the other main suggestions are an auction system for new stock issues (a tender system without a minimum price) and some form of index-linked securities. An auction system is proposed (Griffiths 1979) to force the authorities to give up discretionary control of interest rates. In contrast to the 'tap' system in which new stock is more or less continuously available at set prices, it may lead to more regular month-by-month funding. But it may not provide for the variation in the volume of funding necessary to offset fluctuations in the other components of £M3. This would depend upon how regularly the tender is held, how far in advance details of the auction programme must be provided, and thus how far in advance the authorities must forecast the behaviour of other components. In the USA, there is a set timetable in which two year bonds are offered monthly, and longer terms quarterly. In such a system, it may take one to two months before the authorities are able to vary the programme and thus respond to unexpected money supply variations, whereas these can in principle be immediately offset under present arrangements.

An index-linked gilt-edged security with a coupon interest of 2%, available to pension funds, was introduced at the time of the 1981 Budget. Indexation has had little appeal in the past because the authorities have been wary of an adverse impact upon inflation expectations. Now that there is a government which is making reduction of inflation an overriding priority of policy, it has a different appeal. Worries about the willingness of the public to hold securities in times of rising inflation have been replaced by a concern about the real repayment burden of 10 year or longer securities issued in 1980 at nearly 15%, if inflation does return to single digit figures. The government is saddling itself or its successors with interest payments that can be justified only against continuance of high inflation. This is a further reason why the authorities are examining the issue of more short term debt.

Bank Lending

Because of the unpredictability of gilt sales with the present tactics, and the uncertain impact of policy on the other components, considerable weight attaches to controlling bank lending. Amongst the components it is the immediate province of the Bank. Control over short term interest rates has been the primary means used to influence the growth of bank lending. MLR is pushed up with the expectation of effecting immediate sales of public sector debt, while the

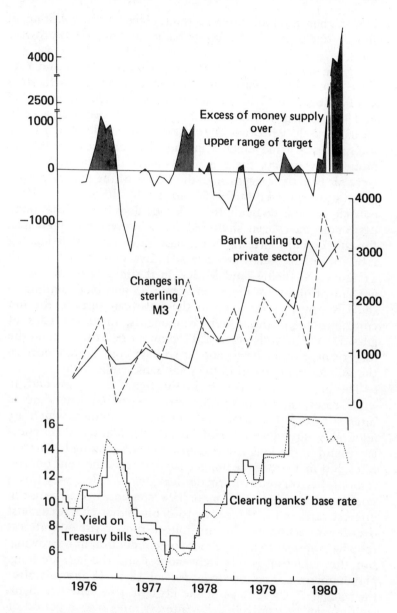

Figure 4.1 *Money Supply Targets, Bank Lending and Interest Rates (£m; and basis points)*

new higher level of interest rates places a more lasting, if slower operating, brake upon bank lending, via borrowing rates.

Figure 4.1 shows the behaviour of M3 for 1976−7 and £M3 since April 1977 relative to the upper target for each. (It is a reflection of how far monetary targets have been exceeded in 1980 that observations after July 1980 could be accommodated only with two alterations to the scale used!) If we interpret sharp movements in the yield on Treasury bills as induced by policy, there is no evidence that the authorities were tardy in their response to the excess of the money supply growth over target in 1976 and 1979, although the 1978 episode is more difficult to read. Nor does it seem that bank customers have been sheltered from interest rate increases, for the London clearing bank base rates (to which lending rates of other banks are related) have moved in line with Treasury bill yields (and MLR). In the middle of the figure are shown quarterly movements in £M3 and bank lending to the UK private sector. From these we can surmise the net contribution of the other components, including sales of gilts. During periods when £M3 grew more strongly than the target, these other items appear to have contributed more to the subsequent correction than has bank lending.

The impression gained from the figure of a slow and, in some cases, an imperceptible response of bank lending to interest rates is confirmed in econometric studies, which are admirably surveyed by Hotson (1979). Marked differences are found in the long run response of bank lending to interest rates, but in all cases the impact elasticity (i.e. the same quarter response) is very low, normally less than 0.1. In a way this is not surprising since the immediate consequence of a rise in interest rates is for the banks to debit higher charges against overdrawn accounts. In the longer run, a rise in interest rates does appear to bring about some reduction in borrowing. But the reduction is relatively modest and the lags are long. Maximum responses occur in general 12 to 18 months after the change. These lags make it doubtful whether bank lending can be controlled by interest rates over a period of less than one year without marked instability of rates.

This slowness of response of bank lending to interest rates

is all the more surprising since the interest rate weapon has been supplemented until recently by application of the 'corset', and the correlation is so close that we can only observe the combined effect of the two. The corset reinforced interest rates by making it more costly for banks to bid for deposits to sustain their lending, thus providing them with a pecuniary incentive to use interest rates more vigorously to choke off potential borrowers. Banks sought to evade the corset by keeping business away from their balance sheets. One of the more visible 'leaks' was bank acceptances. Customers were persuaded to issue a commercial bill, guaranteed by the bank, which the customer discounted for immediate cash in the market. In this way the borrower obtained temporary finance at high cost, and was not refused help by the bank. During the 12 months prior to the abolition of the corset, non-bank holdings of these bills increased by £1,500m. With the removal of the corset in July 1980, much of this business returned to the banks, swelling lending (which increased by £3,000m in July alone) and £M3 (see figure 4.1).[5] In this sense, the 'true' bank lending in 1979 may have been that much greater, and the response to interest rates that much less.

Why is bank lending so unresponsive to interest rates? At least four factors seem relevant. First, most bank lending is to industrial companies. Studies (e.g. Moore and Threadgold 1980) of these companies' borrowing from banks indicates that it is significantly determined by the costs that the firms face. Wages bills, import costs, and tax payments all seem to swell bank borrowing and, as we noted previously, render the money supply partly endogenous to the inflationary process. Circumstances in which the authorities are seeking to restrain monetary growth are typically those in which firms need more finance to meet higher wage bills and imports of oil and other commodities. In short, the attempt to move up the demand curve for loans by higher interest rates is swamped by the shift of the curve. Some would say that this slippage is not undesirable. It ensures that high interest rates do not bankrupt firms facing cost increases over which they have little control. But the demand for funds could reflect other things.

Amongst these other things we note, secondly, that many firms apparently use bank borrowings as a more or less permanent source of funds, now representing about 54% of external funds compared with less than 40% in the 1960s (see table 7.1 p. 134). They borrow from banks because the equity market in the 1970s has been fragile, while the debenture market has suffered because of firms' unwillingness to go into debt at fixed interest rates. By contrast, bank lending rates are flexible, adjusted in line with market trends. Firms may see that they have little alternative but to stay with the banks and take the rough with the smooth. In any case, interest rates may prove to be only temporarily high. Clearly, the 'Duke of York' tactics in the gilts market may lead to the wrong climate of expectations for bank borrowers.

Third, there is the question of whether interest rates really are 'high'. If firms are not induced to switch from bank loans to other avenues of borrowing (equity, fixed interest debentures, money market instruments, trade credit), interest rates must deflate the economy until total borrowings decline. While nominal rates have some significance, expected real rates of interest seem more relevant. In *ex post* terms, the real rate of interest has been negative more often than not since 1974 (see table 4.3). If companies are in a position to offset the nominal interest payments against profits for corporate tax purposes, the post-tax real borrowing costs of bank loans can be even lower (i.e. more negative). These calculations are based on the actual rate of inflation. If the authorities have to judge what *expected* real rates are in order to restrain bank lending, one of the arguments favouring a monetary target is destroyed. We recall that one element favouring a switch to monetary targeting from interest rate targeting was the inability to judge real expected interest rates (see page 41 above).

Fourth, the behaviour of the banks cannot be ignored, especially as companies may accept loans for precautionary reasons in anticipation of greater difficulties in obtaining loans at later dates. It is often said that banks are unable to control their advances portfolio in times of restrictive monetary policy, because customers draw down previously agreed borrowing facilities. Short of cancelling the rights under

Table 4.3 Calculation of Firms' Real Costs of Borrowing (per cent per annum)

	(1) Prime Borrowing Rate	(2) Retail Price Index	(3) Real Rate (1 − 2)	(4) Post-tax Borrowing Rate+	(5) Real Post-tax Rate (4 − 2)
1974	13.0	19.2	−6.2	6.24	−12.96
1975	12.0	24.9	−12.9	5.76	−19.14
1976	15.0	15.1	−0.1	7.20	−7.90
1977	8.1	12.1	−4.0	3.90	−8.20
1978	13.5	8.4	5.1	6.48	−1.92
1979	18.0	17.2	0.8	8.64	−8.56
1980	17.0	15.0	2.0	8.16	−6.16

+ Calculated on the basis of corporation tax payable at 52%.

customers' noses, banks can make the advances more costly, but the usage remains at the customers' volition. In fact, this is a considerable simplification especially in the highly competitive British financial system in which banks compete for the lending business of companies by offering facilities and open credit lines. We can write advances as $A = F(A/F)$ where A is advances, F is facilities and A/F is the usage rate. The increase in bank lending can be written as

$$\Delta A \cong F\Delta(A/F) + (A/F)\Delta F$$

That is, the increase in advances is broken into that coming from changed usage of existing facilities and that from new facilities granted at 'normal' usage rates. We cannot say that one is 'demand' and the other 'supply', but obviously any supply influences operate on the second, which is proximately attributed to new facilities and may account for much of the increase in bank lending.

The question must be asked, then, whether policies to control bank lending are aimed at the correct target. Consideration of this must await an examination of bank intermediation. Meanwhile, we observe that without the 'corset' and the reserve assets ratio, the banks' participation in the control of lending is virtually limited to raising base rates in line with MLR, so that interest rates can operate upon the public's demand for credit. If that fails, their responsibility ends too. Under a system of monetary base control, which has been suggested as an alternative control mechanism, quite different behaviour would be required of the banks.

Conclusion

Under the present 'supply side' approach, increases in £M3 are split into PSBR, sales of gilts, external flows and increases in bank lending, and policy is directed at altering those components. Judging from the extent to which the money supply has exceeded target (see figure 4.1), the results have so far been disappointing, to put it mildly. Apart from spurts in gilt-edged sales, the response of £M3 to interest rate variations appears slow and uncertain. By directing attention to each of the components and away from the total money supply, the markets tend to react adversely when any one component is misbehaving, not appreciating that it may be counteracted by one of the other items. In particular, overruns in PSBR targets have encouraged the authorities to subsume fiscal policy almost entirely to the dictates of monetary control, despite difficulties in containing the deficit in the face of rising unemployment. This constraint upon taxation and expenditure policies, in the name of monetarism, is an indication of how little the authorities feel they can rely upon interest rates to control gilt sales and bank lending.

The low interest rate response of the credit counterparts of £M3 seems to be just as much an inhibition on a policy operating on the 'supply side' as the low response of the margin between government paper and bank deposit rates was to a policy operating on the 'demand side'; the authorities seem to have gained nothing from the change in strategy. But the supply side approach has focused attention on how much the present system relies upon the interest elasticity of the demand for credit for it to work. On one view the low elasticity is a blessing, and the lower is the interest elasticity of a particular aggregate, the better placed it is to be a target. It then necessitates that interest rates be used with a vigour sufficient to alter expenditures and incomes and thus the demand for credit (or money) *indirectly*. The answer, especially after the removal of the corset, is for the interest rate weapon to be used more frequently, more quickly and with greater force. This is the message contained in the Green Paper. On another view, interest rates are an inadequate means of controlling the money supply. Having always to use interest rates or fiscal policy to deflate the economy for monetary control is unwarranted. Other, nore direct, techniques must be explored. We do so after examining the nature of bank intermediation in Britain.

Notes to Chapter 4

1. In Australia, changes in Statutory Reserve Deposits (the equivalent of Special Deposits) act against the fulcrum of banks' liquid and government securities ratio (a controllable equivalent of the reserve assets ratio) to lever away liquidity and thereby enforce reductions in banks' rate of lending. See Davis and Lewis (1980) for a description.
2. Committee on the Working of the Monetary System (1959), Minutes of Evidence, p. 6. HMSO.
3. It is still the authorities' intention for there to be some cash requirement to provide a fulcrum for these operations. However, it is now being extended to all banks and licensed deposit-takers above a minimum size. At the same time the ratio is being reduced to not more than 0.5% of eligible liabilities (see *BEQB* March 1981, p. 38). This extension makes the ratio more readily convertible to use as a mandatory cash ratio under a system of monetary base control.
4. Banks' net foreign currency liabilities are added to eligible liabilities (and the interest bearing components are added to interest bearing eligible liabilities i.e. IBELS), but net assets are not subtracted. Thus banks with net spot foreign currency asset positions could offset their growth in IBELS by switching-in.
5. Another 'leak' was to the Eurosterling market, discussed in Chapter 7.

5

Bank Intermediation

This chapter is not a survey of either bank intermediation or the British financial system. Rather it draws attention to some features of both, prior to a discussion of proposed systems of monetary control in the next chapter. These features also condition the form of prudential controls over banks, considered later in this chapter.

Our starting point is to note that in the money supply £M3, deposits of the UK private sector constitute 83% of the total (as at October 1980) and are the most volatile part. Most of these deposits (75%) are held with the clearing banks. In terms of the credit counterparts of £M3, these banks are less dominant but still provide 65% of sterling loans to the UK private sector.

However, these banks do not dominate the British banking system, as is shown in table 5.1. This gives details of the total deposits of UK-based banks as at January 1980 classified into 3 groups:

(a) the *clearing banks* i.e. the six London clearing banks, the three Scottish clearing banks and the four Northern Ireland banks. These banks form the basis of the payments mechanism and have an extensive network of branches and agencies in the UK.

(b) the *'Other British'* banks, numbering 117 in all. Five of these banks are deposit banks, operating much like the clearing banks, but the others specialise in merchant banking or wholesale banking activities. The merchant banks proper are the accepting

Table 5.1 Deposits of UK-Based Banks, January 1980 (£m)

	No. of Banks	STERLING DEPOSITS						FOREIGN CURRENCY DEPOSITS					TOTAL LIABILITIES
		Total	UK Banks	UK Public	UK Private	Overseas	CDs	Total	UK Banks	UK Other	Overseas	CDs	
CLEARING BANKS													
London Clearing Banks	6	37,979	3,193	481	30,750	2,327	1,229	8,405	2,003	700	5,307	395	55,961
Scottish Clearing Banks	3	4,046	200	80	3,527	103	136	1,126	481	116	419	110	6,534
Northern Irish Banks	4	1,291	513	34	674	70	–	20	9	6	5	–	1,553
Total	13	43,316	3,906	595	34,951	2,500	1,365	9,551	2,493	822	5,731	505	64,048
OTHER BRITISH BANKS													
Accepting Houses	35	3,857	1,118	38	2,210	407	84	5,438	1,518	494	3,305	120	10,397
Other British	69	15,193	6,595	341	5,588	2,008	662	19,795	5,506	635	12,614	1,040	38,953
Discount Houses	13	4,528	4,221	13	242	52	–	82	41	22	19	–	4,796
Total	117	23,578	11,934	392	8,040	2,467	746	25,315	7,065	1,151	15,938	1,160	54,128
OVERSEAS BANKS													
American Banks	62	7,013	3,102	12	1,871	932	1,096	50,670	6,547	1,436	31,182	11,505	58,080
Japanese Banks	22	554	338	–	168	43	6	28,035	7,134	152	17,257	3,493	28,729
Other Overseas	129	6,177	2,596	1	1,267	1,910	402	45,172	8,897	897	32,950	2,428	52,127
Consortium	29	775	519	1	90	133	32	8,570	3,314	96	5,002	158	10,127
Total	242	14,519	6,555	14	3,396	3,018	1,536	132,447	25,892	2,581	86,391	17,584	149,063

houses, which have traditionally financed commerce and international trade via the 'accepting' of bills. Their activities are
now much broader than this and they are involved in money
market activities and longer term lending to industry as are the
specialised subsidiaries of the clearing banks and the UK registered
banks with predominantly overseas business. Also forming part of
this grouping are the discount houses which are pure wholesalers
in short term securities.

(c) the 242 *Overseas Banks*. These are the branches, subsidiaries and
joint ventures (consortia) of banks owned and registered overseas
i.e. American banks, Japanese banks, EEC banks, British
Commonwealth and other overseas banks. Like most of the
Other British banks, these banks have few branches in the UK
and have little involvement in the payments system.

Table 5.1 indicates some marked differences between the
deposit structure of the clearing banks and the much more
numerous non-clearing banks. In terms of sterling deposits,
the non-clearing banks' share is nearly 50%, as compared
with their much smaller contribution to £M3. One factor is
non-resident deposits which are excluded from £M3, but the
main reason is the large amount of interbank deposits (netted
out of money supply statistics) which the non-clearing banks
hold. One of our tasks is to explain why this difference exists.

A second difference is the involvement in Euromarket
(foreign currency) business in London. The clearing banks
stand out (along with the discount houses) as the only group
whose UK business in sterling is less than that in foreign
currency. London has a vast 'offshore' (Euro) banking system
grafted onto and closely connected with the domestic (sterling)
banking system (Revell 1980). This Eurosystem has important
implications for monetary control, as we saw in the previous
chapter, by giving the banks room to manoeuvre their credit
expansion within a monetary target. Without exchange
controls, they are able to lend in foreign currency to domestic
firms or divert sterling lending business to branches in other
Eurocentres. These implications are considered in Chapters 6
and 7. Our immediate interest is the different character of
the banks' business.

Table 5.2 provides other measures of the differences
between the banks. First, most of the non-clearing banks'
deposits are interest bearing and the vast majority of these

Table 5.2 Various Aspects of Sterling Business of UK Banks, February 1980

	London Clearing Banks	LCB Subsidiaries	Accepting Houses	Other British Banks	UK Registered Overseas Banks	Foreign Banks	Consortium Banks
A. Sight Deposits as per cent of Total Deposits	44.09	14.14	27.35	13.50	24.12	18.99	22.13
B. Per cent of A which are Current Deposits	88.12	16.44	14.32	27.78	n.a.	n.a.	13.83
C. Current Deposits as per cent of Total Deposits	38.85	2.32	3.92	3.75	n.a.	n.a.	3.06
D. Deposits with Maturity >7 days as per cent of Total Deposits		24.45	46.66	66.33	60.82	n.a.	68.39
E. Overdrafts as per cent of Total Advances	60.68	5.49	11.77	10.41	14.06	n.a.	1.30

Source: Item A is from *Bank of England Quarterly Bulletin.* Items B to E are based on a sampling of British banks.

are for fixed terms in excess of seven days. Second, of the sight deposits of the non-clearing banks, most are in the form of interest bearing monies at call, not current deposits used for cheque payments. Third, few of the non-clearing banks' loans are in the form of overdrafts, being term loans.

Prior to 1971, these differences begged of a simple explanation: there were two banking systems (Revell 1968). One was a 'retail' banking system, conducted by the clearing banks and the small deposit banks, dealing with households and small to medium-sized firms. The other was a 'wholesale' banking system operated by the other banks. They dealt in large sums with large companies and public authorities, having a relatively small number of customers on both sides of the balance sheets. Wholesale banking was subdivided into international (foreign currency) business and domestic wholesale business, but the two grew up together as the banks serviced the domestic as well as international needs of multinational corporations and transferred staff and skills developed in the Euromarkets into domestic operations.

Different controls were applied to the two systems, and the Bank of England in 1968 doubted whether application of the same liquidity ratio would be appropriate (Bank of England 1968). Revell (1968) asked whether it would not be better to acknowledge the differences and cease to count the deposits of the non-clearing banks as part of the money supply. These worries were swept under the carpet by the 1971 reforms which spread the controls to the non-clearing banks while encouraging the clearers to imitate the practices of the other banks (see Chapter 1).

Now it is the case that we can no longer identify purely retail banks and purely wholesale banks. All British banks are multiproduct firms, operating simultaneously in the different markets and producing different kinds of services. Moreover, the division between retail and wholesale has been broken down by what is termed 'intermediate' business, as some companies move between the two markets in response to credit needs. Nevertheless, the two tables indicate that the weighting of retail and wholesale banking clearly differs between the classes of banks in an identifiable way. Our interest is to examine the two forms of banking and explore the implications for prudential and monetary controls.

Retail Banking

Financial intermediaries operating in the retail market (of which banks are merely one form) must ultimately reconcile the divergent portfolio preferences of borrowers and lenders. Borrowers want to issue long term debt with very simple characteristics (mortgages, share capital, debentures) and have access to short term finance without notice (bank overdraft). Lenders predominantly want securities with a short term to maturity, less default risk and more convertibility, transferability, divisibility and reversibility than they can obtain by holding the primary securities of borrowers. When combined, we refer to these characteristics as 'liquidity'. Banks (intermediaries) in the retail market carry out a transformation process comparable to the technical production processes in manufacturing, in which the primary securities are transformed into deposits which have liquidity. We ask first how liquidity comes about in the system as a whole and then in individual banks.[1]

Lenders' (i) supply of funds is assumed to be an increasing function of interest return and liquidity,

$$F_i = F_i(r_i, L_i) \tag{10}$$

where L_i denotes the liquidity provided to ultimate lenders. Borrowers (j) are assumed to value illiquidity (long maturity loans, repayment at convenience with overdrafts etc.) so that the demand for funds is a decreasing function of interest return and liquidity (L_j),

$$F_j = F_j(r_j, L_j) \tag{11}$$

Ignoring transactions costs, banking results in a difference in liquidity to ultimate lenders and ultimate borrowers, i.e.

$$L_p = L_i - L_j \tag{12}$$

This excess L_p is produced by the banks expending costs on real resources (labour, capital and materials) and incurring liquidity costs in terms of the income foregone from holding reserves. For simplicity, assume that the costs of producing liquidity services (C_p) depend upon the amount of transformation:

$$C_p = p(L_p) \tag{13}$$

With competition, banking services will be expanded until

$$r_j - r_i = C_p'; \tag{14}$$

that is, until the marginal cost of net liquidity, C_p', equals the marginal valuation which lenders and borrowers place upon it. This is indicated by the interest differential which in combination lenders sacrifice and borrowers pay.

The manner in which individual banking firms produce liquidity has been treated in two ways in the literature. Both ways accept that banks must hold cash (currency and bankers' balances at the central bank) since they provide deposit (and loan) facilities which have uncertain maturities, and cash is also needed for interbank settlements (transferability) and to enable convertibility into currency. Some writers treat this demand for cash (or base money or high-powered money) as a reserve constraint. An ordinary productive firm maximises profits subject to a balance sheet constraint and a technical production function relating the scale of operations to inputs of capital, labour and materials. These constraints also face the bank firm, but the peculiarity is an additional reserve constraint, part of which consists of base money. Other writers treat base money as a direct input into banks' production function. Banks are visualised to purchase primary assets, pool them to eliminate risks and combine them with high-powered money, capital, labour and materials to create a claim which has special characteristics. Amongst the characteristics desired are convertibility into cash and transferability in the settlement of debts, both of which require inputs of high-powered money.

In both cases, reserves held are a fraction of deposits. Not that the principle of fractional reserves is peculiar to banks, for it is employed by any business which borrows against future income and converts what is borrowed into another form. What is different about banks (and other retail intermediaries) is that insurance principles can be used to determine the size of reserve holdings needed to 'insure' against the risks of deposit withdrawals. By using the law of large numbers, banks can balance the marginal returns from additional investments against the costs of running out of reserves. An extensive literature exists to describe how an individual bank balances these factors and determines its asset portfolio. In a sophisticated money market with an efficient interbank market and many cash substitutes, holdings of base money may be very low. But, according to the theory, there is a determinate reserve demand which limits acquisition of non-reserve assets. It is this lever which would be used under a system of monetary base control to restrain banks' credit creation.

So far we have treated (retail) banks like any other retail intermediary (e.g. building societies, savings institutions) ignoring their involvement in the payments mechanism and any differences which come from acceptance of their liabilities as money.[2] One implication of this acceptance is their use as the principal means of payment and reserve asset of other retail intermediaries. Hence, in Britain, non-bank intermediaries (and non-clearing banks) typically hold bank deposits as primary reserves, while clearing banks hold base money. It is this difference which gives rise to the 'pyramid of credit' conception. A transfer of deposits to other intermediaries can have as its *immediate* consequence a change in the ownership of deposits, not in their total. Depending upon acquisitions of public sector debt by the other intermediaries, an indirect extinction process is then substituted for what would otherwise be, and is for other intermediaries, a direct loss of deposits (Llewellyn 1979a). The more significant difference comes from the distinction between acceptance and demand. Bank liabilities are accepted, but may not be demanded except as a 'temporary' abode of purchasing power' between transactions, because they can be used later for buying goods and making other payments. Deposits can come into existence without the receiving banks having to offer higher inducements and commit the resources and reserves needed to service them. For banks as a whole, there is a short run divergence between the costs of having increments to deposits accepted and the costs of retaining them, for they constitute 'money on the wing' not 'money sitting', to use Robertson's (1922) happy terminology.

Thus the differences between bank and non-bank intermediation come from the short run disequilibrium processes which characterise the market for money and underlie the supply side analysis of money creation. Neither individually nor collectively do banks 'gain' from this in the long run, since by definition it is a feature only of short run disequilibrium. But the difference does give the banking sector a special significance in transmitting monetary disturbances to the real sector, and does influence the choice of monetary control technique.

Wholesale Banking

The one distinguishing characteristic of wholesale banking is the comparatively large size of the units in which business is transacted. Several other characteristics follow from this. Wholesale bankers typically have a small number of large customers, whereas retail banks in a branch banking system number theirs in the hundreds of thousands or even millions. It follows that wholesale banks cannot utilise the law of large numbers to determine optimal holdings of reserves. What is the basis of their intermediation?

One theory is that wholesale banks provide services which are quite different from those of retail banks; they spread liquidity but do not produce it.[3] An absence of maturity transformation is assumed, banks (and lenders and borrowers) dealing in securities of the same type and term to maturity. Wholesale banks follow the principle of 'matching' their liabilities and assets, in the sense that all loans of a particular maturity are financed by deposits of the same maturity (Revell 1968). In this way, they obviate the need for reserves.

According to this theory, 'transactions costs' (widely defined) are the basis of banks' existence. In the retail model, we ignored transactions costs but allowed for differences in liquidity. Here we assume $L_i = L_j$ and focus on transactions costs. The supply of funds from lenders is now

$$F_i = F_i(r_i) \tag{15}$$

where r_i is the interest return, net of transactions costs. Borrowers' demand for funds depends on the total cost of loans; that is, interest plus transactions costs, *viz*

$$F_j = F_j(r_j) \tag{16}$$

In the absence of banks, firms would solicit loans from each other and face various transactions costs. Common to borrower and lender are brokerage fees, search costs, communication costs, and costs of recording and administering accounts. Lenders face the additional cost of obtaining information about borrowers and assessing their credit-worthiness. These costs drive a wedge between the net interest return to lenders and the total cost paid by borrowers, even though the transacted interest rate is the same for both. Denoting the market clearing rate as r, the net interest return on the last loan transacted is

$$r_i = r - t_i \tag{17}$$

where t_i are the marginal transactions costs of lenders, and the cost to borrowers of the last loan concluded is

$$r_j = r + t_j \tag{18}$$

where t_j are the marginal transactions costs incurred by borrowers. Thus,

$$r_j - r_i = t_j + t_i \tag{19}$$

In equilibrium, the interest rate differential between the cost to the borrower and the return to the lender reflects the sum of their marginal transactions costs.

Financial intermediaries in general and wholesale banks in particular may possess a comparative advantage in processing loan transactions, acquiring information about borrowers and in monitoring bills of exchange and such market instruments, for three reasons. First, banks may be able to achieve economies of scale from specialisation. Second, most banks have a reputation for discretion when investigating credit-worthiness. Third, banks may be able to reduce the geographical costs associated with search. Ignoring any costs of dealing with banks, they are able to enter the market so long as their transactions costs are less than the sum of t_j and t_i.

With competition, r_j would tend to fall and r_i rise as funds are channelled from lenders to borrowers at lower cost and thus more efficiently when routed through the banks. From (15) and (16) we should expect the entry of banks to be accompanied over time by an expansion of borrowings and lendings even if the overall (average) level of interest rates is unaltered.

Should the cost of direct transactions between borrowers and lenders be large, while that between banks be low, the funds may pass from ultimate lenders to ultimate borrowers via a number of banks, some specialising in tapping deposits, allowing others to specialise in lending. This is the position in the sterling wholesale market. The clearing banks and other deposit banks channel more funds to the non-deposit banks than is the reverse. In foreign currency operations in London, the US banks perform a similar role and channel funds in dollars to British banks for on-lending.

In this model, the *raison d'être* of banks lies in their ability to distribute funds more cheaply than in direct financing. By assumption, the banks balance the maturity of their liabilities and assets. They exchange securities without really changing their basic characteristics. Because they do not create liquidity, they have no need for reserves or holdings of base money.

While matching is an important facet of wholesale banking, the margins to be had now from straight brokerage or rerouting operations are not large, and a bank that was perfectly matched would soon go out of business. Banks can get wider margins by 'riding the yield curve' and taking advantage of interest rate differentials in the term structure of interest rate. If it is the case that $r_j^S < r_j^L$ and $r_i^S < r_i^L$ so that $r_i^S < r_j^S < r_i^L < r_j^L$, where the superscripts S and L denote short term and long term securities respectively, then banks can obtain the largest interest differential by combining r_j^L with r_i^S, and undertaking lending which is of somewhat longer maturity than their borrowings.

In this second theory of wholesale banking,[4] banking behaviour is linked with theories of the term structure of interest rates, for it relies upon factors outside the banking system influencing the yield to maturity pattern. If expectations about future short term rates are the dominant influence, a bank expecting to profit from mismatching backs its judgment of interest rate movements against those of the other transactors: undertaking positive maturity transformation if, in its view, the long term rate exceeds compounded present and future short term rates, negative maturity transformation if it is less. Either could occur, but in fact positive maturity transformation prevails. As it seems unlikely that bankers' views would consistently deviate in one direction from the market's view, we must ask why there is a premium upon short term funds (or a discount upon long term funds). Uncertainty about interest rates is one factor. Prices of 'longs' fluctuate more than prices of 'shorts' when there is an equal change in yields, so that the holding of longs offers the possibility of greater gain but risk of greater loss. If the market is averse to risk, but banks are not or are less uncertain about the direction of interest rates, they can profit from others' uncertainty and risk aversion. They balance the expected gains from mismatching, in the form of a wider interest differential (net of transactions costs), against the risks from interest rate variability which arise from an open position. This open position can be covered by holdings of marketable securities since matching is still the rule and banks are mismatched only to the extent necessary to profit from interest rates; there is no need for holdings of cash.

If this and the previous model are valid descriptions of wholesale banking, then Revell's question as to whether these deposits should be included in the definition of money seems appropriate. Liabilities seem likely to be only a little more liquid than assets and only a little more interesting than the intercompany-type activities they replace. While this form of intermediation is an important facet of wholesale banking, it is far from a complete picture. Our contention is that wholesale banks now undertake considerable maturity transformation.

Some idea of the extent of the maturity transformation can be gained from 'mismatch curves' for the foreign currency and sterling operations of British banks. Like Lorenz curves, the mismatch curves (pioneered by Hewson) are calculated by expressing the percentages of assets and liabilities in each maturity class as a percentage of the totals, cumulating the

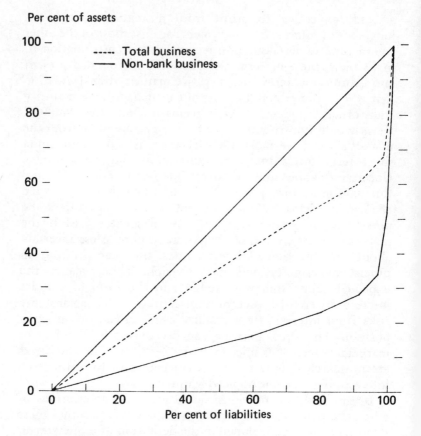

Figure 5.1 *Mismatch Curves for British Banks in Foreign Currencies* (as at February 1980)*

*Data are cumulative proportions, calculated as term to maturity increases

percentages. Perfect matching is given by the diagonal. The extent of mismatching is given by the area enclosed between the curve and the diagonal. Figure 5.1 gives the maturity distribution of the foreign currency (Eurocurrency) assets and liabilities of British banks, based on data published by the Bank of England. No comparable data are available of sterling liabilities and assets. A sampling of selected British banks,

Per cent of assets

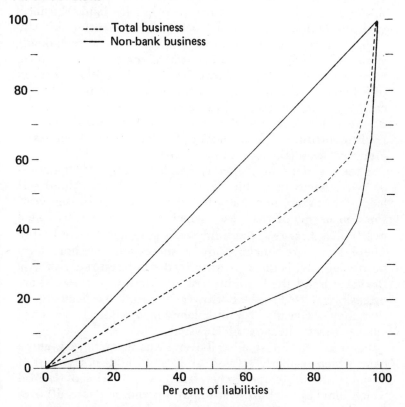

Figure 5.2 *Mismatch Curves for Sample of Selected British Banks in Sterling* (as at February 1980)*

---

*Data are cumulative proportions, calculated as term to maturity increases

engaged mainly in wholesale business, is collated and presented in similar fashion in figure 5.2. From discussions with members of the banking community it would seem that the sample is reasonably representative of the wholesale balance sheets in sterling of many other banks in London.

Two features stand out. First, both figures show, even for the total balance sheet, an excess of liabilities over assets at the short end of the scale, conversely at the long end. When interbank claims are netted out to reveal the banks' business with the non-bank sector, a much greater extent of maturity transformation is evident. Second, there is a remarkable similarity in the degree of mismatching between foreign currency and sterling business. We may be entitled to speak of characteristics of 'wholesale' intermediation', whether carried out in Eurocurrencies or in domestic currencies. One of the writers has argued elsewhere that the two may effectively constitute a single market for international wholesale intermediation (Davis and Lewis 1981).

Based on the sample, nearly one half of the sterling assets of 'wholesale banking business' consists of loans. About one half of loans are nominally for terms in excess of one year, some in excess of five years, which are renegotiated ('rolled over') on a three or six monthly basis at variable interest rates. These loans are financed by a succession of short term borrowings. With these provisions, the 'interest rate risk' (via flexi-rates) and the 'liquidity risk' (via optional renewals) are ostensibly shifted to the borrower. Indeed, it has been argued that they are really 6 month loans in a relatively matched balance sheet (Niehans and Hewson).

In practice, almost all roll-over loans are renewed, and a bank which regularly refused to do so 'would soon go out of business', to quote one banker. It is the expectation of renewal which induces the borrower to pay a premium ('spread') over 6 month money. What otherwise determines the term structure of interest rates under flexi-rates? Any tendency for yields to rise with maturity (the normal course of events) cannot be attributed to capital gains and losses on fixed nominal rate securities. Our argument is in terms of transaction costs, with borrowers paying a premium to have guaranteed renewals and to avoid the transactions costs inherent in financing medium term loans themselves by a succession of short term instruments.

On this interpretation, banks in wholesale markets are undertaking maturity transformation, although probably to a lesser extent than in retail banking. But the major contrast with retail banking is not the extent of the transformation, but the manner in which it is performed. While retail deposits

can be withdrawn upon demand or at short notice, in practice
they are not all withdrawn at once. The same stochastic
principles cannot be applied to wholesale deposits. Matching
of maturities and currencies is the rule, but how are loans of
3 or more years to non-banks matched with deposits of very
short term maturities?

Our contention is that the interbank market performs a
'fiction' which allows liquidity creation to occur in wholesale
banking. It may do so in 2 ways:

(i) Wholesale Bank *A* receives a large deposit. It seeks out
     some non-bank customers, and lends the rest to Bank
     B via the interbank market. Bank *B* in turn loans out
     some to non-bank customers and the rest to Bank *C*
     etc. This method of sharing out the transformation can
     be done in this informal way or formalised in the
     consortia principle and in syndicated loans.

(ii) Wholesale Bank *C* is approached for a loan by a non-
     bank customer on a 6 month roll-over basis and bids
     for 3 month interbank funds (liability management).
     Bank *B* supplies a 3 month interbank loan, itself
     accepting 1 month money from Bank *A* which has
     received a call deposit.

In one or both of these ways, each bank is mismatched, but
not to any great extent, so that no one bank is left with a
large share of the transformation process. In retail operations
the transformation is undertaken *fully* by the bank which
accepts the deposits. In wholesale markets, some or all of the
transformation is undertaken by the system.

Two implications follow from this third theory of wholesale
banking. If banks in wholesale markets were large enough
relative to the customers they could conceivably utilise
stochastic principles, in which larger banks are always better
off than smaller banks. Tendencies to concentration in
domestic markets, as evidenced by mergers amongst Dutch
and French banks, and the dominance of the three largest US
banks internationally, can be attributed in part to wholesale
activities. Secondly, and reinforcing this insofar as the clearing
banks are concerned in Britain, a bank which operates in
both retail and wholesale markets should possess advantages

over one specialising in either area. They can rely upon a stable retail deposits base for most wholesale lending, limiting their use of more expensive wholesale deposits for topping up. By a judicious mix of business, either risks can be lowered or returns increased.

Since the risks which face banks in wholesale markets differ from the risks in retail markets, we now assess the implications of these theories for prudential controls, noting that most banks operate to some extent in both markets.

Prudential Regulation

Prudential regulation refers to actions by the central bank to ensure that banks and other financial institutions maintain adequate capital reserves and adequate liquid resources to meet their obligations in domestic and foreign currencies. As part of the '1980 reforms' the Bank issued discussion papers on 'The measurement of capital', 'Foreign currency exposure', and 'The measurement of liquidity' as a preliminary to instituting a new set of prudential arrangements.[5] Final details have not been worked out, for the proposals have not been well received in the City. Supplemented by the release in 1981 of a further note 'The liquidity of banks' (*BEQB*, March 1981), they stand now as a guide to the Bank's view about how controlled institutions should and do operate. Although these documents originated from different parts of the Bank, they are linked with the Green Paper on Monetary Controls because of the Bank's view that the area of monetary control and prudential supervision must coincide and because, at the margin, the two types of control shade into each other.

While our main interest is this connection with monetary control, we ask why prudential regulation is needed, what institutions are to be supervised, who is responsible for them, and what form the regulation is to take? The need for intervention arises because it is costly and difficult for the market to assess an institution's ability to meet its contractual commitments. Yet the social institution of money rests critically upon public confidence in banks. One person accepts the banks' promises to pay because there is confidence that others in turn will find them acceptable. Adequate supervision is one way of maintaining confidence, by ensuring that the promises to pay become actual receipts.

In retail markets, institutions themselves provide for their own safety by utilising the law of large numbers to determine the size of reserves needed to 'insure' against the risks of withdrawal (illiquidity) and to determine the amount of equity capital needed to 'insure' against default of loans (insolvency). Illiquidity and insolvency in fact differ essentially in their time horizons, liquidity being concerned with the availability of funds for the continuity of business, while solvency is concerned with the resources available to repay creditors in the event of liquidation (Revell 1975). Where this type of 'insurance' differs from other insurance is in terms of confidence. Withdrawals are random, independent events only if depositors have complete confidence in the institution concerned. Once confidence is shaken, nothing short of 100% reserves may suffice, and the failure of one intermediary may impose considerable externalities by undermining confidence in others. Thus regulation has its main justification in preventing the event insured against, rather than in recompensing disaster victims.

Wholesale banking has, if anything, added to these potential instabilities. Revell (1978) argues that runs on banks are more likely to begin with wholesale depositors who are the first to hear rumours of impending trouble. The more competitive banking system which often accompanies the growth of wholesale banking makes for instabilities. Much of the 1973–4 fringe banking crisis in Britain can be traced to competitive forces unleashed by Competition and Credit Control. As the clearing banks recovered business from fringe bankers, the latter were forced into progressively more speculative business in search of profit. Because of the peculiar way in which maturity transformation is undertaken in wholesale markets, via the interbank market, there is the chain risk that a few defaulting loans can rebound through the whole banking system. (Interbank markets can create a further element of risk. Whereas an individual bank may deem it prudent to limit the share of its advances placed with a particular customer, funds placed 'interbank' may eventually end up with that customer).

Only governments and central banks can ultimately

guarantee the liquidity of claims in nominal terms. This (often implied) guarantee reduces the importance of gearing and reserve ratios in perceptions of the intermediaries' safety and thus is of considerable commercial benefit to the institutions' shareholders. Governments may properly require some *quid pro quo* from the banks. This could take very simple forms, e.g. a specific levy on each pound of deposits related to the riskiness of the chosen portfolio, were it not for 'moral hazard'. An institution may seek to take advantage of the guarantee by continually sailing close to the wind. Prudential supervision is needed to ensure that last resort support is not the first line of defence, so that the public at large are not bearing risks which should rightly fall upon the institution's shareholders.

Prior to the Banking Act 1979, supervision was exercised informally by the Bank over the primary banking sector. There was no comprehensive statutory definition of a bank and a proliferation of banking names occurred. A number of companies which found themselves in difficulty in the fringe banking crisis were deposit-taking institutions not regarded as banks by the Bank and *ipso facto* not subject to its supervision. This was the situation which the Act sought to remedy by requiring those wishing to take deposits from the public, unless exempted (as the building societies and trustee banks have been), to apply to the Bank for permission to do so either as 'banks' or as 'licensed deposit-takers' (LDTs). Both sets of institutions are to be supervised by the Bank. So far the Bank has signalled that its intention is that both are to be treated equally for the application of prudential and monetary control, the latter necessitating an eventual revision to the definition of money. Otherwise institutions within the arrangements could avoid credit control and prudential obligations by channelling business through associates which lie outside the sector.

In a financial system as complex as that in Britain, a desire for equity may be akin to the search for the holy grail. Equality of treatment does not imply equality of controls imposed. Not only do LDTs differ from recognised banks, as their different status acknowledges, but the mixture between retail/wholesale and domestic/international business differs markedly between banks. This influences desirable prudential (and monetary) controls.

Complications flow from the Euromarket operations of banks. With so many of the banks being branches and subsidiaries of foreign banks, there is the question of who should be responsible: the regulatory authorities of the country in which the banking institution operates (the 'host') or those of the country from which the institution comes (the 'source'). Table 5.3 sets out the recommendations of a Committee of Central Bankers (Blunden 1975). These are only recommendations and meanwhile host countries' authorities must supervise both liquidity and solvency. They also look to the foreign currency position, for banks are exposed to exchange rate risk insofar as they do not 'cover' every loan or deposit in a particular currency. Previously, exchange control regulations limited a bank's open position. In their absence, a bank's own prudence will, and does, lead it to limit its exposure to exchange rate fluctuations. Although the Bank's additional requirements are still under discussion, it seems likely that they will restrict a bank's open position in each currency and in aggregate in relation to its capital base as defined in the 'Measurement of Capital'.

Rather than discuss the liquidity and capital proposals in detail, for they are yet to be finalised, we note several implications of the theories outlined earlier. Simple ratios of liquid assets to deposits and of equity capital to loans and investments accord with retail operations of banks in which the law of large numbers can be applied to many items. Specified requirements for these do not, of course, guarantee safety, for only reserves and resources in excess of the requirement can be used (Harrod's cab rank fallacy — see Harrod

Table 5.3 Areas of Primary Responsibility Recommended by Basle Committee of Banking Supervisors 1975

Form of Foreign Establishment	Supervision of Liquidity	Supervision of Solvency
Branch	Host + Source	Source
Subsidiary/Joint Venture	Host	Host

1969). For wholesale operations more complex arrangements are required, because holdings of reserves will be conditioned by the structure of the balance sheets and the extent of mismatching maturity by maturity. Both papers recognise this. The capital paper proposes arbitrary coefficients for capital cover reflecting the relative risks of the different categories of asset, with cash having a zero weight ranging through to property loans with a weighting of 2.0.

The same idea appeared in the liquidity paper. For determining liquid assets cover, the balance sheet is divided into three categories: (1) maturity uncertain assets and liabilities (e.g. sight liabilities and overdrafts); (2) maturity certain assets and liabilities (e.g. time deposits and term loans); (3) interbank deposits and interbank standby facilities up to 1 month. For items (1) and (2), the liquid assets cover which is proposed depends on the mismatched position and the term to maturity. (For example, on 7 day liabilities net of 7 day claims the suggested cover is 90%, on 6–12 month net liabilities the suggested cover is 15%).[6] In the case of (3), assessed in *gross* terms, 100% cover is proposed! Given the critical role which is played by the interbank market in 'reconciling' the public's preferences with those of the banks and allowing maturity transformation to occur (at least in our theory), the enactment of such norms could constitute a severe tax on wholesale intermediation. Following adverse reactions from the banks, these precise proposals seem likely to be softened. However, the Bank evidently still wishes to pursue the notion of calculating a single figure of liquidity cover, presumably on similar principles to those used in the original paper.

The Bank's reason for the interbank proposal was that a lower coefficient 'would enable banks to create illusory liquidity through interbank transactions'. But all liquidity is, in a sense, illusory. In retail business, the primary securities which 'back' deposits are not really altered by the transformation process. Banks cannot insure themselves against total loss. Accordingly, a distinction must exist between situations in which one bank is short of cash and can be helped by other banks and those in which the system as a whole is under pressure. In the latter case there must be a range of assets which the authorities buy for cash or lend against (last resort loans).

But banks are short of cash for two reasons. One is the exercise of convertibility, the other is the application of monetary control. The Bank's view has been that the conflict between these is irreconcilable. That is, the existence of a pool of assets which the authorities are prepared to accept in return for cash, in order to protect the system's safety, militates against any form of monetary control centred upon the authorities controlling the cash available to the banking system, which is what monetary base control is about. We examine this, and other forms of monetary control in the next chapter.

Notes to Chapter 5

1. Pyle (1971), Mangoletsis (1975) and Niehans (1978, pp. 166—70), examine the conditions which are needed for liquidity creation to occur. We follow the analysis of Mangoletsis. Klein (1971), Towey (1974), Saving (1977), Sealey and Lindley (1977), Niehans (1978, pp. 175—82), and Baltensperger (1980) examine the way liquidity is created by individual banks.
2. These differences are surveyed in Coghlan (1977) and Lewis (1980a), which give earlier references.
3. This function is emphasised most in analyses of the Eurocurrency market, see Hewson (1975), Niehans and Hewson (1976), Freedman (1977) and Weston (1980). The possible importance in domestic markets is mentioned in Benston and Smith (1976) and Baltensperger (1980).
4. See Niehans and Hewson (1976) and Niehans (1978).
5. References are given in Chapter 1. The papers are critically reviewed by Blanden (1980), Lomax (1980) and Wood (1980).
6. As a 12 month fixed deposit eventually becomes a 7 day deposit, this means that the cover required on net liabilities varies over the 'life' of the deposit. See Wood (1980).

6

Methods of Monetary Control

The Green Paper of March 1980 was prompted by worries about the precision of existing monetary controls. It reviewed various techniques without coming to any firm conclusions as to the inadequacy of existing procedures or the desirability of new methods of control. In the circumstances of 1980—81, as judged by the extent to which monetary targets have been over-shot (see Table 3.1, p. 40 and figure 4.1, p. 69), these conclusions seem unduly complacent.

Our discussion, as in the Green Paper, groups the techniques which can be used to control the money supply under three headings:

(i)   direct controls, in the form of reserve requirements such as the 'corset' and Special Deposits;
(ii)   interest rate control; and
(iii)   monetary base control.

Monetary base control can be effected by open market operations and the same is true when interest rates are the control mechanism. In this case, techniques (ii) and (iii) are frequently grouped together as 'market' policies, although they are different in their application. Monetary base control is a quantitative restriction upon banks' balance sheets which operates via market mechanisms; interest rate control is a cost restriction operating via the market.

One omission from this list is the use of moral suasion, which consists of requests for the banks to adopt voluntarily certain restrictive (or expansionary) measures that conflict with their immediate self-interest. They are encouraged to comply, in the national interest, for the sake of good relations with the central bank, and because of the central bank's ability to discipline them by using direct controls. Suasion is easier the smaller is the number of banks, for several reasons. It is easier to recognise individual acts of non-compliance. Use of direct controls when suasion fails imposes costs on all banks; but when spread over a large number the penalty for a non-complier is reduced. Finally, moral suasion has been described as an exchange of co-operation by banks for information from the central bank, and information is more easily transferred via informal meetings with a small, homogeneous group of bankers. As the British banking system has grown in size and complexity, the value of suasion has been reduced. The formalisation of prudential controls, discussed in the previous chapter, is a recognition of this fact. Nevertheless, suasion is still used. A recent example was the agreement by the banks to refrain from using the Eurosterling market to bypass the corset controls when exchange controls were lifted in 1979.

Direct Controls[1]

Reserve requirements differ in operation from open market operations in two main respects: first, they seem likely to produce different consequences for the structure of interest rates; second, they can 'tax' intermediation. Open market operations are implemented by changes in the *supply* of government interest-bearing debt relative to private sector debt. Alterations to reserve requirements are implemented via banks' *demand* for government and private sector debt. There is no reason to expect the time sequence and pattern of interest rates which result to be the same. In general, one might expect open market operations to exert more of an impact upon government interest rates, and changes in reserve requirements to have a larger relative impact upon private sector interest rates. Different consequences could follow for output and prices. Any differences here may exist even if the tax effect of a reserve requirement is absent.[2] The tax effect comes about because the constraint upon banks' acquisition of non-reserve assets inherent in a reserve requirement can impose pecuniary costs which influence the scale of intermediation which it is profitable for them to undertake.

Consider an intermediary which is maximising expected short run profits under competitive conditions, without controls. Intermediation is assumed to expand until zero expected profits are earnt on the 'last' funds transformed. The anticipated net yield on loans is obtained by adjusting the loan rate (i_L) for expected default, where β is the difference between posted and effective interest rates due to default risks. Included in the asset portfolio on prudential grounds is a proportion (α) of reserve assets earning the interest rate i_A. Costs include not only the interest rate on marginal deposits (i_D) but also the capital, labour and material costs, where a is the 'administrative' costs per pound of marginal funds. Each firm seeks a level of operations which equates (short run) marginal revenue (r) and marginal cost (c): that is, where

$$c = r \qquad\qquad (20)$$

where $c = i_D + a$

and $r = (1 - \alpha)(i_L - \beta) + \alpha(i_A)$

As with any other firm in the economy, monetary policy can impinge upon the operations of the financial intermediary in two basic ways (although we examine later whether monetary base control offers a third mechanism). One is by purchasing or selling stocks of commodities and so bringing about changes in relative prices generally which alter the marginal-revenue/marginal-cost conditions facing the intermediary. This is the basis of the interest rate control mechanism, implemented via open market operations, considered in the next section. The other is by taxation. Consider a call to Special Deposits. The intermediary must place a fraction (s) of its asset portfolio (assumed equal to total deposits) into a special account at the Bank of England at the rate (i_s) and the remainder $(1-s)$ is then invested in the other assets (including the reserve assets) with a net yield (r) at the margin. Hence the new equilibrium is

$$c = (1-s)r + s\,(i_s)$$

$$= r - s(r-i_s) \tag{21}$$

So long as r (and c) exceeds i_s, the call widens the gap between the cost of marginal funds and the net yield which is sufficient to ensure that the marginal funds can earn profit. In the second expression, the first term on the right hand side is the net expected marginal return from liability incurrence when there is no call to Special Deposits while the second term $s(r-i_s)$ indicates the marginal opportunity cost imposed upon the incurring of liabilities due to the call. (We assume that the intermediary's own demand for reserve assets does not contract by an amount equivalent to the Special Deposits call).

It follows that we can view Special Deposits as a 'tax' upon intermediation, the tax base being eligible liabilities and the tax rate equal to $s(r-i_s)$. The effectiveness of the tax is governed by the size of the call and the interest rate differential $(r-i_s)$. When the tax is effective, some contraction of the scale of the intermediary's balance sheet from that in (20) is required to raise r (or lower c). This contraction in turn forces actual and would-be borrowers to use more costly and more inconvenient finance from untaxed non-bank intermediaries and from a reversion to direct financing ('disintermediation'). If the tax persists, these alternatives become less costly and less inconvenient; usage makes them better substitutes. Direct controls thus promote the development of alternative untaxed sources of finance, and reduce the relative market share of the taxed intermediaries.

At present British banks are subject to two direct controls: Special Deposits and the 1.5% cash ratio applied to the clearing banks. The point of the latter is to make clearing banks' holdings of monetary base more predictable and is soon to alter in form (see Chapter 4). Special Deposits are used partly because of the announcement effect and because they are a means of quickly impounding banks' surplus reserves. Here the aim is to contain bank lending, preventing inflows of liquidity from leading to 'secondary' expansions of deposits. Neither control is valued for the tax effect, which in any case is very small. Special Deposits earn banks the Treasury bill rate. When they were in operation in December 1979, the call was 2% of eligible liabilities. With a prime lending rate of 18% and Treasury bill rate of about 16%, the tax was only about 4p per £100 of marginal private sector funds transformed. The combination of Special Deposits and the 1.5% cash ratio resulted in a tax of about 30p per £100 to London clearing banks (at these rates), on the assumption of an unchanged excess cash reserve ratio.

Application of the corset (Supplementary Special Deposits) was a different matter. It introduced an additional differential between a bank's marginal loan and deposit rates. Furthermore, the differential rose sharply as a bank moved beyond the allowable growth of interest bearing eligible liabilities (IBELs) from a base date. Under the arrangements introduced in June 1978, for example, Supplementary Deposits became payable if an institution's average IBELs for the three months August—October 1978 grew by more than 4% over the average for the six months November 1977—April 1978. The rate of deposit was progressive in three tranches, according to the extent of the excess. We denote each tranche by:

$$\gamma_0 = 0 \qquad \text{(Corset off)}$$
$$\gamma_1 = 0.05 \qquad \text{(First tranche, less than 3\% excess)}$$
$$\gamma_2 = 0.25 \qquad \text{(Second tranche, 3—5\% excess)}$$
$$\gamma_3 = 0.50 \qquad \text{(Third tranche, over 5\% excess)}.$$

Moreover, unlike ordinary Special Deposits, the Supplementary Deposits earned the banks *no* interest. Consequently the equilibrium becomes

$$c = (1 - s - \gamma)r + si$$
$$= r - s(r - i_s) - \gamma r \qquad (22)$$

Comparing (22) with (21) we can see that a bank forced into the third tranche would then have to more than double its asking rate on a marginal loan for it to be profitable to bid for an additional interest bearing deposit.

A form of control like the 'corset' is likely to impinge

more upon wholesale banking activities than upon retail banking for several reasons: margins are finer, there is a greater reliance upon interest bearing deposits, and large corporate customers have a greater ability to bypass the banking system. This is not surprising; the corset was specifically introduced in December 1973 (and continued to February 1975) to make it costly for banks to bid for wholesale deposits. Since then the scheme has been in effect from November 1976–August 1977 and June 1978–June 1980. By the last occasion the distortions it induced had become obvious. Two practices reduced its effectiveness (Griffiths 1979). First, banks engaged in window-dressing transactions in anticipation of the imposition of the corset. This involved expanding their IBELs much faster than £M3 in order to start off in the corset with an artificially large base of IBELs, which could then be run down. Just prior to June 1978, IBELs were increasing at an annual rate of 25%, whereas £M3 was increasing at 15% per annum. This was in spite of a warning from the Bank that the corset would be backdated and they would not gain (Pepper 1979). In the event, the corset was backdated but perhaps by not enough to discourage similar pre-emptive transactions if there was to be a next time round.

These anticipatory actions enabled many banks to sustain their lending and thus their contribution to £M3 during 1978–9 without coming within the corset provisions. By 1979–80 this buffer had gone but the 'bank acceptance' leak grew, as banks helped customers to shift their borrowings to the money markets in the form of commercial bills; 'disintermediation' occurred. In the words of the Green Paper, 'to the holder, such bills are no less liquid than a certificate of deposit of comparable term, and to the borrower they are a very close substitute for direct bank credit' (p.5). It was the potential for such disintermediation, as well as the possible Eurosterling leak (marginal banking operations being shifted 'offshore'), which led the Bank of England to abandon the corset as a means of credit control.

The case against direct controls should not be overstated. If bank acceptances are nearly as good as bank lending, why did 're-intermediation' occur in July 1980 when the corset was lifted? Similarly, the idea that bills are as good as bank deposits ignores the fact that 30% of wholesale deposits are at call and 90% are for maturities of less than 3 months. Because of the extent of maturity transformation now undertaken by the banks in both wholesale and retail business (see Chapter 5), re-intermediation like that in July 1980 is not without effect. Furthermore, some disintermediation is almost inevitable in any policy which restricts the growth of banks' balance sheets, as borrowers are forced to resort to more expensive non-bank finance. This process is one way in which restrictive policy is transmitted from the banking system to other financial markets. So long as interest rates restrain expenditures, the credit restriction remains. Direct controls encourage more disintermediation to occur, depending upon the time horizon over which they apply. Whether this is good or bad needs to be judged against how well other control techniques work. In any case, it can always be argued that even when the effect of the control is largely cosmetic, appearances are sufficiently important in monetary affairs that such an effect should not be despised.

Bank and Non-Bank Responses to Interest Rates

Under the system which was supposed to operate after 1971, direct controls like the corset were not meant to be the sole, or even the major, instrument of monetary policy. That role was assumed by interest rates. They were to exert a 'generalised influence on credit conditions' spread across banks, non-bank intermediaries and the parallel money markets. In this way, disintermediation and the dilution of controls over time would not arise.

It was expected that banks would react to a credit restriction by raising lending rates (so as to moderate the demands on them for funds) and also deposit rates (so as to obtain more funds). The interaction of a reduced demand for funds and a rising marginal cost of funds supplied was supposed to bring about an adjustment of bank and non-bank balance sheets via market mechanism. When the system was put to the test in 1973 a problem emerged: lending rates rose much less than deposit rates, so much so that CD rates exceeded loan rates and round-tripping occurred. The corset was originally designed to put a stop to this state of affairs by exerting a sharp added pressure on trading margins. Subsequently, its application sought to provide an appropriate backdrop against which the interest rate weapon could successfully operate. It was hoped that the presence of the corset would encourage banks to raise their lending rates more forcefully, so making interest rate control more potent, and/or induce them to take steps to limit their credit-giving more directly. In the event, the banks seem not to have responded in the first of these ways and this has added to the difficulties encountered with interest rate control.

In order to examine these difficulties we return to the theme developed in Chapter 1 of the different responses to policy of major groupings of financial intermediaries. This particular way of looking at the behaviour of the financial sector corresponds more closely with the retail/wholesale distinction drawn in the last chapter, for marked differences exist between the intermediation of deposit banks, other (non-deposit) banks, insurance and pension funds, and other non-bank institutions (mainly building societies and savings banks) — the four groups distinguished. Previously, we examined these groups' incurrence of liabilities during the 1950s and 1960s. We now look at responses since 1971, based on Lewis (1980b).

Figure 6.1, covering the period 1971 to 1980, graphs the quarterly seasonally adjusted increases in liabilities of the four groups to the UK non-bank private sector, along with MLR, taken as an indicator of policy. Three periods can be identified when the authorities were actively seeking to restrain the growth of liquidity by interest rate increases, supported by the corset: in 1973—4, 1976 and 1978—9. In all three episodes, the same pattern emerges. The liabilities of insurance and pension funds show some inverse response to interest rates but, as might be expected, it is much less than that of the other non-bank group (building societies, finance houses, investment and unit trusts, and savings banks). Liabilities of the latter group appear to respond promptly to interest rates. But the major contrast is with the liabilities of

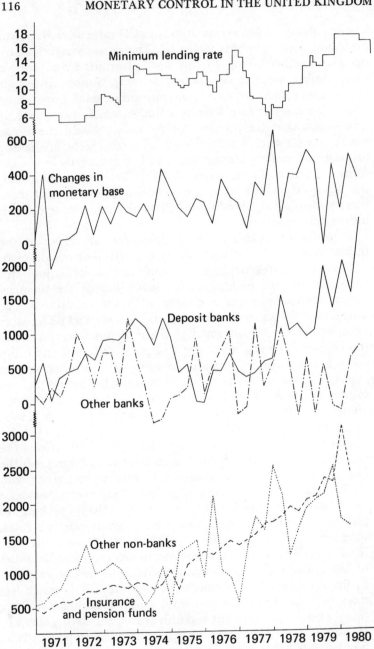

Figure 6.1 *Incurrence of Liabilities by Major Financial Groups and Monetary Policy Indicators, 1971–80 (£m or base points)*

the banking groups. Changes in the liabilities of the non-deposit banks show evidence of an inverse relationship with interest rates. It is the liabilities of the deposit banks which do not. They eventually appear to slow down in response to higher interest rates, but the response is less immediate and much less than that of the other banks.

Some figures for 1979 illustrate the point. In that year monetary growth pushed against the upper limit of the target range and intermediation was under the influence of a 7 percentage point increase in MLR. Non-deposit banks' liabilities to the UK private sector increased by only 2% over the year. Deposits of the building societies and the savings banks increased by 11%. Those of the deposit banks expanded by 20%! Bank lending to the UK private sector reflected these differences, although not to the same extent (because of on-lending facilities via interbank markets). Loans and advances by deposit banks to the UK private sector increased by 23%, those of other banks by 13%.

Interestingly this differential response is contrary to the longer run trends in which the non-bank groups are expanding more rapidly than the deposit banks. It is also in contrast to the first two years of the new system (competition *without* credit control). Only with greater credit control, and higher interest rates, has the pattern changed. What is also interesting is that the pattern is almost the exact opposite of that which we observed for the two previous decades (figure 1.1). In the 1950s and 1960s, when direct controls were the main instrument, the exercise of restrictive policy appeared to fall directly upon the deposit banks. The impact upon other banks and the non-banks was less and slower to operate. In the 1970s, with greater use of interest rates, the 'other non-banks' responded first, followed by non-deposit banks and then, and to a lesser extent, the deposit banks. It is tempting to say that a system of controls which placed the burden of restrictive monetary policy upon the clearing banks and little upon other institutions has been replaced by one which does the opposite. But to reach this conclusion we must be able to explain why the various groups respond differently to the interest rate weapon.

The reasons for the different responses of the two non-bank groups seems clear. Insurance and pension rights are geared to income and future considerations, and are unlikely to be sensitive to interest rate changes which are expected to be short-lived. By contrast, the possible vulnerability of savings institutions to swings in monetary policy features in policy discussion in many countries. It can arise if there is a slow adjustment of their rates to market yields so that the net inflow of funds drops off when interest rates rise. Building societies change rates on existing as well as new loans, which makes changes costly (because of the potential default risk when loans are of a credit foncier sort) and politically controversial. They are mutual organisations and as people deposit funds in order to qualify for loans, a demonstration of reluctance when raising loan rates is warranted. Whether this reluctance will continue in the future, as the building societies evolve like banks and the trustee savings banks actually become banks, is of some concern to the authorities. In 1980, the Financial Secretary to the Treasury warned the societies that if they began bidding for money market funds like the banks, the government would reconsider their exemption from the provisions of the Banking Act.

Turning to the behaviour of the two banking groups, we must ask why the non-deposit banks are more sensitive to interest rates or, equivalently, why the deposit banks appear to be less responsive to interest rates. Since the non-deposit banks' business is almost entirely wholesale, while that of the deposit banks is a mixture of retail and wholesale, it would seem likely that the reason for any differential response lies in the character of their intermediation.

In comparison with retail (or mixed) banks, wholesale banks rely upon 'buying' interest bearing funds in corporate and interbank markets, which may dry up as interest rates rise, but in addition the nature of their balance sheets and associated risks could be important. An 'interest rate risk' arises if banks are 'taking a view' about interest rates and relying upon borrowings shorter than holdings of securities and the rollover period on loans. In the latter case, they face a profits squeeze over the intervening period until loan rates are re-negotiated. If interest rates are expected to rise (or rise further), banks will be expecting an erosion of their profits and capital losses on holdings of marketable securities such as bills, bonds and certificates of deposit. They will endeavour to lengthen their liabilities and shorten their assets. Failing this, they may prefer to unwind their portfolios in advance of the increase in interest rates. If policy is able to induce this expectation, this form of bank intermediation may respond relatively quickly to monetary policy.

Reinforcing this is the 'status risk'. Because of the critical role which the interbank market plays in wholesale banking (see Chapter 5), banks seek to protect themselves (and the market) from the chain risk of defaulting loans echoing through the system by the use of 'names' and credit ratings. With nearly 300 banks participating in the market, it relies upon information of a bank's position being passed around. One index is the margin by which a bank's interbank offer rate exceeds that of first-class names. If a bank's status is lowered a tier and its margin raised, this can sometimes be passed onto the borrowers at rollover date, but the loss of status is then publicised more widely. Refusal to renew the loan is not really a viable option, since the borrower is 'paying' for the commitment and in any case may not be in a position to repay. A bank in this position may wish to avoid entering the market too often or for too large an amount, preferring to effect adjustments within its asset structure rather than 'liability-manage'.

If this is an appropriate description of wholesale banks' intermediation, then credit transformation by deposit banks is quite different. Whilst they also engage in wholesale banking, their distinctive feature is the provision of liquidity and payment services. The appropriate model is one of liquidity creation, as in retail banking. On the asset side, the liquidity services take the form of overdraft facilities and short term accommodation at attractive interest rates, the usage of which is primarily at the customer's volition. All the factors examined in Chapter 4 which have led firms to rely more extensively upon bank lending than in the past impinge more directly upon the deposit banks than upon the others. Any failure of interest rates to deter borrowings from deposit banks assumes significance because their liabilities are used as 'money'. There is a demand for them for payments as well as to hold, and they will be accepted, even if not demanded, as a temporary abode of purchasing power between transactions. Deposits can come into existence or be extinguished (for example because of changes in advances) without interest rate inducements or disincentives. This distinction between temporary and permanent holdings of money makes banks' intermediation qualitatively different from that of other institutions.

These inherent differences explain much of the different behaviour, but not all. Why don't deposit banks, caught between a rising demand for loans and the penalties of the corset, raise loan rates to levels which choke off loan demands? After all, this is how they are expected to behave. It may be true that banks' first inclination nowadays is to bid for more deposits to support loans rather than 'asset manage'. It is also true that deposit banks normally raise rates on existing as well as new loans. Both of these statements are really descriptions and not explanations, since the practices could change.

As we have described the system, banks have to be short run profit maximisers if the appropriate pattern of interest rates is to be brought about. This is not a good description of the banker—customer relationship in retail banking, nor of the fierce struggle for market shares in the highly competitive British banking system. Banks like to cultivate profitable long run relationships with their clients, even if this means foregoing some short term profit. Moreover, the clearing banks continue to enjoy a partial collusive monopoly in the retail business. For both reasons, the implicit interest rates which the banks pay on current accounts adjust only slowly to market forces. As earnings on the asset portfolio rise, there is an endowment effect on profits arising from the large current account deposit base (see table 5.2). The banks are able to deploy this endowment as, in effect, a subsidy to marginal loss-making business in time deposits. Because of the endowment effect, banks may be quite capable of maintaining their borrowers in difficult times, through bidding for funds at loss-making rates of interest, and still show higher profits than at low rates of interest. Moreover, this behaviour allows them to avoid the charge of profiteering by charging higher interest rates (though, if the loss-making business is not big enough, they may still expose themselves to an excess profits tax — as in the March 1981 Budget!)

But the general lesson is that a market-based system of controls can work only if the participants are presented with stimuli appropriate to the way they operate. If bank customers are not daunted by high interest rates, banks see no alternative but to bid for deposits and reserves to sustain their intermediation. In the 1950s and 1960s they were prevented from doing so by interest rate ceilings. In the 1970s, the process was made more costly by the corset. Both 'solutions' are now unpalatable to the authorities, and the measures of 1980 seem designed with the aim of shaking existing rigidities like overdraft charging practices out of the system. In effect, the participants have to change to suit the authorities' preferred system of monetary control. Might it not be better to change the system? It is in this context that we examine proposals for monetary base control.

Monetary Base Control[3]

Although the Green Paper was intended to examine monetary base control (and any other possible systems) as an alternative to present arrangements, it failed to get to grips with the real issues involved. It consistently identified monetary base control merely as a means of triggering changes in interest rates ('a means for the markets to generate the *interest rates* necessary to bring the rate of growth of the money supply back towards the desired path'). Nor surprisingly, the conclusion was reached that the authorities would do just as well, if not better, by bypassing this step and adjusting interest rates directly to money supply deviations, as is done at present. What is ignored is the possibility that control of the money supply via the monetary base is different from interest rate control, as was stated by Milton Friedman (1980b) to the Treasury and Civil Service Committee of the House of Commons.

> Direct control of the monetary base is an alternative to ... interest rates as a means of controlling monetary growth. Of course, direct control of the monetary base will affect interest rates ... but that is a very different thing from controlling monetary growth through interest rates.

If monetary base control is different, we must ask how it

works and provide a frame of reference for evaluating its costs and benefits *vis-à-vis* interest rate control.

Such a framework is provided by the theory of a banking firm involved in liquidity production (see Chapter 5). In the standard theory, control of the money supply can be achieved by control of the growth of base money provided that banks adhere to a stable (excess) cash reserve ratio. Base money is of importance to banks because they need it to provide for the convertibility and transferability of deposits, and in case open credit lines and unused overdraft facilities are drawn down. Banks can be visualised as purchasing primary securities, pooling them to eliminate risks and combining them with capital, labour materials *and* base money to create liquidity. They are able to employ the law of large numbers to keep cash at low levels, but cannot eliminate the need for cash completely. As a bank lends or invests, the loss of cash puts it in a position where any subsequent deposit withdrawals or loan demands may necessitate sales of securities at a loss or interbank borrowings at unknown rates. These possible costs must be balanced against the benefits of increased income. In this way, the availability of cash limits banks' acquisition of non-cash assets.

Control of the money supply is exercised by restricting the quantity of the factor input, base money, into the banks' production function. Since the monetary authorities have a monopoly over the production of this factor input, they can make it available in less than perfectly elastic supply: in the limit, the supply could be made perfectly inelastic. Banks are then in the same position as firms in any industry for which the inputs required for production are available only at sharply increasing cost. For an individual bank, the restriction of the supply of base money imposes an external cost as banks in the system expand deposits and bid for reserves. (Each bank's supply response is a mixture of a movement along a short run cost curve and a shift of that cost curve as rising factor prices impose an external pecuniary diseconomy). An individual bank can react in a variety of ways: by bidding for interbank funds, raising deposit (and loan) rates, improving services, cutting back on new facilities, cancelling or reducing existing facilities, selling CDs, disposing of bills or bonds. The route actually chosen will be the one most profitable to the bank.

One immediate difference from the interest rate mechanism now operated is the involvement of the banks. Following the removal of the corset, the banks are almost passive spectators in the process of monetary control. Their 'job' is to raise interest rates, but that is about all. The Bank of England, as it were, appeals directly over their head to the public's demand for credit. If borrowers are not daunted by higher interest rates, the banks bid for deposits and reserves to sustain any expansion of advances. Monetary base control, by contrast, impinges directly upon banks' decision making and provides a pecuniary incentive for them to participate in the process of adjusting their balance sheets to the dictates of monetary policy.

A second difference concerns the adjustment mechanism. Under monetary base control the mechanism would be chosen by the banks on profit-maximising grounds. At present, the form of the adjustment (e.g. interest rates operating upon credit demand) is chosen by the authorities. If that fails, the authorities must either raise rates further, or wait for credit demands to subside. Until the latter eventuates, banks are supplied with cash to prevent them running out of reserves. Left to themselves, banks could well choose to respond to a reserve shortage in the same way — by raising deposit and loan rates. Should interest rates fail to restrain the demand for money or credit, this could not be the end of the matter. A reserve deficiency would still exist and banks would be forced to try something else. They always have the alternative of disposing of earning assets to the non-bank private sector, leaving total deposits unchanged. Some assurance would exist that the adjustments would proceed until monetary growth came into line with the growth of base money.

The idea that there is some new breed of banker who will always eschew asset management for liability management is patently false. If interbank rates are bid up high enough, it would pay some banks to sell bills and bonds to the private sector in order to obtain funds for lending out in the interbank market. Liability management is allowed to succeed because the Bank provides the reserves needed to validate deposit expansion.

Perhaps the most important difference is in terms of the implications for behaviour next time round. Once banks are forced to make up reserve shortages by borrowing interbank at 'penalty cost' or by selling securities at a loss, they are likely to exercise much greater care in future when granting facilities and open credit lines. Unused facilities are a valuable source of liquidity to customers, and banks might, in different circumstances, be expected to vary the 'price' for this service. There would also be an incentive for banks to refrain from lending and build up reserves when reserve shortages are anticipated. Accordingly, surges in monetary growth may be less likely to occur.

In this description, monetary base control *is* qualitatively different from interest rate control. At the aggregate level it operates by imposing a quantitative restriction upon banks' intermediation. This is translated directly into individual banks' profit calculus. Friedman summarises the differences as follows:

> Trying to control the money supply through 'fiscal policy and interest rates' [to quote the Green Paper] is trying to control the output of one item (money) through altering the demand for it by manipulating the incomes of its users (that is the role of fiscal policy) or the prices of substitutes for it (that is the role of interest rates). A precise analogy is like trying to control the output of motor cars by altering the incomes of potential purchasers and manipulating rail and air fares. In principle, possible in both cases, but in practice highly inefficient. Far easier to control the output of motor cars by controlling the availability of a basic raw material, say steel, to manufacturers — a precise analogy to controlling the availability of base money to banks and others.

Three questions must be asked of monetary base control. First, how inelastic is the supply of base money to banks? Second, does monetary base control constitute a tax on the banks concerned? Third, how appropriate is control of base money to all banks in the system? We consider these in turn.

There are four sources of base money insofar as the banks are concerned: the authorities, overseas, the non-bank private sector, and the banks themselves. Base money can be obtained via lender of last resort facilities, and this has always been seen by the Bank to militate against monetary base control. But last resort loans are only for seven days and a further distinction must be drawn between the availability of assistance and the price at which it is given. Under the present system the terms of assistance are declared in advance and there is a divorce between the provider and the institutions whose behaviour is to be adjusted. An alternative is for assistance to be given directly at rates decided 'on application'. There needs to be some uncertainty associated with last resort loans because behaviour next period is not independent of how generously reserves are supplied this period. Second, branches of foreign banks operating in Britain could obtain 'last resort funds' from head office. The parent could conceivably buy sterling, lend the proceeds to the branch and thereby relieve its reserve shortage at a cost which is conditioned by the exchange rate risk. Effective control of base money is eroded unless movements of forward and spot exchange rates make the transaction more costly than usage of local facilities. Third, banks could raise interest rates and induce the public to deposit cash, so altering the currency ratio and the 'money multiplier'. Figure 6.2 shows that the real *per capita* currency holdings have fluctuated considerably during the 1970s, but the ratio of currency to the money supply has been reasonably stable and indicates little apparent responsiveness to interest rates. How it might behave under pecuniary incentives, particularly if banks offered customers more than face value on deposits of cash, is another matter. Fourth, banks themselves hold reserves of base money (cash and balances at the Bank of England) and these could be squeezed in the case of need. In practice, given the level of interest rates, it seems unlikely that (excess) holdings would be large, although they would certainly be larger than under present arrangements, for cash would no longer be supplied so willingly. At present, the size of banks' holdings is a very fine lever indeed with which to attempt to control banks' asset expansion (see below). These uncertainties about the size of banks' holdings under a different regime and the elasticity of sources of base money from the public and overseas mean that base control is far from mechanical.

For restraint upon cash to be an effective control device, it is not enough that its supply be inelastic, as is witnessed by the idea of using negotiable licences to control banks' deposit expansion.[4] As with base money, the supply of negotiable

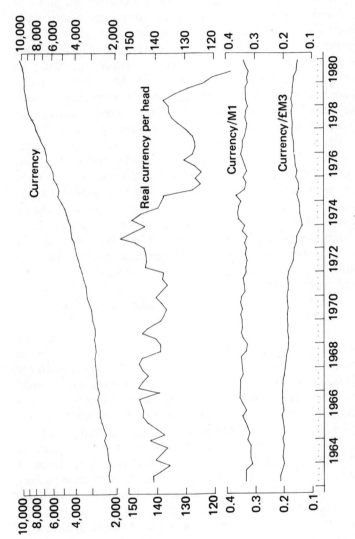

Figure 6.2 *Currency Holdings of the Non-Bank Private Sector (£m in nominal and constant prices and ratio to money supply)*

licences would be monopolised by the authorities. As banks expand beyond allowable limits, variations in the market price would raise costs against individual banks. Yet it is generally agreed that such a scheme would encourage banking to be done outside the controlled area — particularly in offshore markets. Would the same consequences follow from monetary base control? If banks' holdings of base money were involuntary, as under a mandatory requirement, this might well be the case. But, if the theory is relevant, banks' demand is a voluntary one based on a production function for liquidity services, not an arbitrary restriction upon an institution designated to be a 'bank'. Institutions in the Eurosterling market providing substitute liquidity services would require inputs of high-powered money, just as is the case in domestic markets. What competitive advantages would they have over domestic banks to be able to attract the deposit and reserves needed for liquidity production? Much the same question must be asked of the idea that non-banking intermediaries in domestic markets would provide substitute liquidity services, although this view depends upon stability of another reserve ratio — that of non-bank intermediaries.

But are liquidity services the distinguishing characteristic of money? If they are, then perhaps one-third of £M3 should be excluded from the definition. This is a conservative estimate of the amount that represents wholesale funds of the non-bank private sector, most of which is held in banks which specialise in wholesale banking. If they are not excluded then we must ask whether monetary base control is relevant to their intermediation. Wholesale banking is characterised by less maturity transformation by individual banks, and a greater concern for liability management. Where asset and liability portfolios are closely matched, the bank has little need for reserves. In the less extreme case, where maturity mismatching occurs, reserves play a more important role but these are of marketable securities and depend upon the mismatching, maturity by maturity, not upon some scale measure of deposits. It is in fact the case that the non-deposit banks' holdings of base money are virtually zero (see table 6.1). A further comparison comes from figure 6.1 (p. 116), which

Table 6.1 Cash Reserve Ratios of British Banks at 20th February, 1980

	Notes and coin in tills (£m) (1)	Balances with Bank of England (£m) (2)	Cash Balances (£m) (3)=(1)+(2)	Eligible liabilities (£m) (4)	Cash Reserve Ratio (%) (3)/(4)
London Clearing Banks	838	560	1,398	30,055	4.65
Scottish Clearing Banks	460*	—	460	3,267	14.08
Northern Ireland Banks	28	—	28	1,124	2.49
Accepting Houses	1	1	2	2,279	0.09
Other British† Banks	37	10	47	7,079	0.66
American Banks	2	1	3	4,753	0.06
Japanese Banks	—	—	—	359	—
Other Overseas Banks	9	1	10	3,623	0.28
Consortium Banks	1	—	1	335	0.30

Notes:
* Scottish clearing banks hold Bank of England notes to 'cover' their own issues of notes.
† This category includes five deposit banks.

shows quarterly seasonally adjusted changes in the monetary base. The monetary base equals currency circulation with the public, currency held by the banks, bankers' balances at the Bank of England, and Special Deposits at the Bank of England, extended for reserves released from, or called into, Special Deposits (Brunner and Meltzer's 'extended base' concept).[5] Incurrence of liabilities by the non-deposit banks shows little relationship to movements in the monetary base, whereas the liabilities of deposit banks appear to vary more in line with changes in base money. (This visual evidence is confirmed by regression analysis.)

Restraint upon the supply of base money seems likely to curtail retail banking and those substitutes for retail banking which involve the production of liquidity services using inputs of high-powered money (or, in a pyramid of credit, claims against retail banks). If, as we have argued, wholesale banking involves different services and different production processes, it is unlikely to be constrained directly by monetary base control. To vary Friedman's analogy it may be like trying to control the production of metal *and* plastic containers by restricting the input of steel alone. Wholesale banks are affected by monetary base control only insofar as they find the cost of acquiring funds to support their lending has increased. While the markets are linked by (among other things) the interbank market, and the cost of funds on this market will increase as 'retailers' find their reserves squeezed, the lags likely to be involved suggest that any desired response may be more quickly achieved by operating directly with reference to interest rates. Yet, as we have argued, reliance upon interest rates alone, without concomitant control over base money, may have little direct impact upon retail banking.

Conclusion

Monetary base control is usually discussed as if base ('quantity') and interest rate controls ('price') were simple duals, one of the other. With sufficient abstraction this is so. But the point we have tried to establish above is that the nature of the banking system and the different types of intermediation to be found within it in fact suggest that there is much more to it than this.

Of course, it is not possible simply to 'exogenise' the monetary base by *fiat*. In this respect Friedman's 'precise' analogy in terms of the physical control of stocks of raw material inputs is not helpful. It is more as if the stocks of materials were auctioned off. At the margin, the base would have to be kept on track by open market operations, calls to Special Deposits, and restriction of access to the discount window, hence changes in interest rates would be involved and these, perhaps, might be very substantial. But here the interest rates are a consequence of operations required to keep the base 'on track', rather than the other way round. Merely pushing up interest rates without at the same time restraining cash sufficiently is not enough. But any system of monetary base control must have the dual objective of imposing a *quantity* constraint upon deposit banks' intermediation and a *price* constraint upon other institutions, the latter occurring as actions to restrain high-powered money raise interest rates.

In these circumstances, advocacy of one or the other money control mechanism is misleading. So long as monetary base control is more relevant for retail activities and interest rates more relevant for wholesale banking, both are pertinent. Guidelines can be conceived of for the various categories of business, yet the complex interaction of the categories makes it extremely difficult to formulate simple rules for controlling an expanded money supply embracing these components. They are essentially problems of a complex and sophisticated banking system.

Comments by the authorities, and the set of measures introduced in November 1980, indicate that they may be moving towards such a mixed system of control — making interest rates more flexible, yet at the same time publishing data of the monetary base and collecting statistics for estimates of a retail—wholesale division of banking activities, preliminary to paying more regard to the supply of cash to the banking system.

In the meantime, money supply control seems to be in a state of suspense. Although the monetary target for 1980—81 was overshot by a considerable amount — the annual growth of £M3 to mid-February 1981, even after allowing for the return of business caused by the removal of the corset, was some 17.5% compared with a target range of 7—11% — this is being allowed to stand. That is, base drift is being permitted to occur by starting the target of 6—10% for 1981—2 from the inflated February 1981 figure. Rather than persevere with high interest rates, the authorities seem to be hoping that the factors which have pushed financing into the banks in 1979 and 1980 will moderate as the 1980s progress. We examine this, along with some other longer run issues of monetary control, in the next chapter.

Notes to Chapter 6

1. This section has benefited considerably from comments by Kevin Davis of the University of Adelaide.
2. Funds placed in the reserve requirement could be paid a 'market' rate of return, yet changes in the requirement would necessitate that banks alter their demands for non-reserve assets.
3. There is now a very extensive literature examining monetary base control in the British context. A range of views can be obtained from Coghlan and Sykes (1980), Congdon (1980a), Foot, Goodhart and Hotson (1979), Lewis (1980c), Lomax (1980), Griffiths (1979) and Wood (1979).
4. Duck and Sheppard (1978) proposed the control of the money supply by the issue of special reserve deposits available only to banks and which it is mandatory for them to hold. The negotiable entitlements scheme examined in the Green Paper is a derivative of this idea.
5. A release of Special Deposits enables a given amount of base money to be used more intensively by the banking system to support lending. The extended base concept (which is used by the Federal Reserve Bank of St. Louis in the USA) captures this liberating effect. Calculations of the monetary base given by the Bank in the *BEQB* March 1981, ignore this important element.

7

Some Problems of the 1980s

Hardly anyone predicted in advance the inflation, exchange rate and monetary control problems of the 1970s and it would be foolhardy of us to attempt to put a crystal ball to the 1980s. In this concluding chapter we therefore confine ourselves to just two issues. First, we revisit the problem centring round monetary control via interest rates; second, we go on to discuss more generally the problem of monetary control in a world of ever-increasing financial integration. A particular policy aspect of the latter problem is represented by the initiative behind the European Monetary System (EMS), a part of the arrangements of the EEC from which the UK stays for the moment largely isolated, but in which she may become more heavily involved in the future.

Bank Lending, Fiscal Policy and Monetary Control

Where several elements contribute to monetary growth, and are interdependent, it is inappropriate to single out any one element as responsible for monetary growth. Nevertheless, it once used to be fashionable to identify a one-for-one relationship between the PSBR and monetary growth; more recently it would be possible to identify a similar relationship between changes in bank lending and changes in the money supply (see table 4.1 above). During 1980, for example, bank lending to the UK private sector increased by £10,027m and the money supply by £10,897m, the latter well in excess of the target.

A number of 'cyclical' elements added to the upsurge of bank lending in 1980, among which high wage settlements and the high value of the exchange rate are singled out by the Bank of England as important (*BEQB*, December 1980). Maintenance of interest rates on loans of 18% or more, as prevailed for much of 1980, are seen now as exacerbating this position, if only because of the amount of interest debited to accounts, but also by driving firms further into their banks in recessed conditions. Indeed, it is now being said that lower interest rates may aid immediate control of the money supply in several ways: by lowering the exchange rate, and improving the competitiveness of industry; by reducing interest debited to bank accounts and interest payments on newly issued government bonds; and by sales of public sector debt, bought in the expectation of capital gains if rates fall further.

Where these views leave monetary control if the upsurge continues, or is later renewed, is unclear. For 1981–2 the authorities seem to be looking to an abatement of company borrowing from banks as price and wage inflation slows down, and unemployment continues. As Johnson (1980c) so aptly notes, this is tantamount to admitting that inflation has to be reduced *before* bank lending and thus the money supply is able to be brought under control! It hardly needs pointing out that the authorities are meant to control the money supply in order to control inflation.

It is not only for technical reasons that interest rates have seemed to be a flawed instrument of control. High interest rates work through the mortgage market to impact on a politically sensitive area; government's aversion to high interest rates helps provoke a search for alternatives. A tight fiscal policy, reducing the PSBR, is seen as one of these. But this, too, helps reduce the supply of money and inflation by reducing demand, both for goods and for money, first. Moreover, the pursuit of a declining PSBR target can be positively destabilising since the PSBR responds positively to the onset of recession as tax revenues fall and payments of unemployment benefit rise. Just as with the bank lending rates, the suggestion seems to be that the supply of money can be controlled only by reducing the demand for it.

Monetary base control may be viewed, as outlined in Chapter 6, as constraining the supply of reserves to the banking system and inducing banks both to sell other earning assets as advances expand, leaving deposits unaltered, and to exercise restraint in the new loan facilities they offer. This way of putting it affords some distinction in principle between monetary base control and the other methods, though the contrast is of course much less than complete; in particular, the interest rate implications of monetary base control may prove no more acceptable to the authorities than those of present methods and the control may indeed be implemented only as a variation on the theme of control via interest rates, as suggested in the Green Paper.

It is possible that the authorities may be looking for longer run developments in the structure of corporate finance to mitigate some of these problems. One of these developments would be for companies to borrow by issues of debentures and equity rather than borrowing from the banking system. Table 7.1 shows the source of funds of industrial and commercial companies during the 1970s as compared with the 1960s. In the first half of the 1970s there was a sharp drop in internal funds from undistributed profits and firms relied extensively upon 'external' financing, mainly from banks. (External financing in this context means external to the firm.) External financing later in the decade returned to more normal levels, but the much greater recourse to bank credit

Table 7.1 Sources of Finance for Industrial and Commercial Companies, 1964–79, £m

	1964–7	1968–71	1972–5	1976–9
Internal Funds	11,208	16,154	28,471	61,980
External Funds	4,746	7,817	22,168	25,789
of which (%)				
Bank Borrowing	37.3	39.5	55.9	53.6
Shares, debentures, loans	48.3	33.9	16.6	16.1
Credit Received	—	5.8	8.9	12.8
Overseas Finance	14.4	20.8	18.6	17.5

Source: CSO, Economic Trends (various issues)

remains. Issues of equity are out of favour because of the low market valuation of shares relative to current replacement values of assets and because, under present tax arrangements, it may seem a relatively expensive source of funds (at least, for companies returning profits). Since the end of 1976, more debentures have been redeemed than issued (Bank of England 1981).

While uncertainty about inflation and the course of interest rates continues, firms are likely to remain less than willing to issue long term debt at fixed interest rates (McMahon 1981). Worse, if companies believe in the eventual success of the governments' anti-inflation strategy, any issues now would be at a rising real interest cost. Few companies have issued floating rate notes and, failing a lead from the government on indexation, they have preferred bank finance at floating rates. If this demand for bank financing is sustained, can any economic recovery be accommodated if the money supply targets are to bear down upon inflation?

How much of a conflict there is depends in part on the behaviour of the other components, especially the PSBR. It is planned to be reduced so as to 'make room' for private sector loan demands. But an alternative is to alter the aggregate used for the monetary target. An M1 target allows for bank lending to occur provided it is not financed from current deposits. A broader aggregate such as PSL2 allows bank financing to grow at the expense of financing by savings banks, building societies and the issue of money market instruments. An intermediate position between these could exclude longer term liabilities from the definition of money. This is done already with the definition of eligible liabilities, which excludes deposits with an original maturity in excess of two years. Although the two year dividing line is arbitrary, its intention is to draw a distinction between short term deposits and those having more of the character of loan capital. For the London clearing bank groups, as at February 1977 about 2% of sterling deposits were for maturities in excess of one year. Based on our sample as at February 1980, it would seem that only 2.1% of British wholesale banks' deposits were for periods longer than three years. By contrast, 35% of loans were for periods longer than 3 years. If longer term deposits could be made non-transferable, their exclusion from £M3 would allow the banks to fund additional lending to industry from this source with less liquidity creation than occurs at present.

It is, of course, possible for the banks to expand lending within the monetary targets if non-resident sterling deposits continue to grow rapidly and if residents take advantage of freedom from exchange controls to hold their 'money' in the form of foreign currency deposits rather than sterling. In both instances, and especially the latter, the value of the £M3 target has to be questioned.

Exchange Controls and Monetary Policy

Exchange controls are frequently viewed merely as a technique for conserving international reserves without accepting the exchange rate consequences of the decision; that is, as a means of influencing the 'trade-off' between reserve changes and exchange rate changes. It follows that the abolition of exchange controls is likely to 'worsen' the trade-off by increasing the cost, measured by the deviation of the exchange rate from the level desired for the international competitiveness of British industry, of achieving a money supply target. (Conversely, the cost of achieving an exchange rate target in terms of monetary deviations is increased).[1] The new tax legislation introduced in the 1981 Budget, which enables the authorities to tax the interest on foreign deposits, indicates that the government may be having some second thoughts. A similar tax is operated in Switzerland and it amounts to a substantial negative interest rate on foreign deposits, applied to deter inflows of capital which may increase either the money supply or the value of the Swiss franc.

But exchange controls have a more fundamental role of guaranteeing sovereignty over the production of the national money supply. As we noted in Chapter 1, exchange control regulations are a form of protection to domestically located money producers, because many banking activities are either capable of being 'externally produced' or are akin to 'tradeable goods'. Externally produced goods are those produced in

one location and consumed elsewhere. With banking, trans-
portation costs are low and there is no reason in principle
why wholesale banking (and perhaps some retail banking) in
sterling cannot be conducted from Brussels or Paris. In fact,
it already is — the Eurosterling market. In addition, deposits
which UK residents are now permitted to hold (with banks in
the UK or banks abroad) denominated in the major Eurocurrencies ($US, DM) are like tradeable goods. From the
viewpoint   of   holders,   they   are   accepted   and   thus
can be 'consumed' in different locations. From the viewpoint
of banks, they can be produced in different locations. Via the
facility of swap transactions, the deposits can be converted
into lending in any desired currency for which forward markets
exist. We examine first the Eurosterling market, and then
foreign currency deposits.

A Eurosterling deposit is a claim denominated in sterling
on a bank outside the UK, and a Eurosterling loan is a
sterling asset held by a Eurobank. These claims may be with
banks, or a non-bank, and with UK residents or overseas
residents. These definitions are analogous to those of Euro-
dollars, but the issue for Eurosterling is complicated by the
'satellite' nature of the market. Because of the thinness of the
market, a Eurobank in, say, Brussels receiving a Eurosterling
deposit has usually not sought to find a sterling borrower,
nor increase its working balances in London. Rather, it has
sold sterling spot, held the funds in US dollar assets and covered
forward. Similarly, a bank which is requested to supply a
Eurosterling loan would typically 'manufacture' the currency
by borrowing US dollars and 'swapping', that is, buying
sterling spot and selling forward. Eurosterling can always be
created in this way, independently of funds from the domestic
market, and rates are normally quoted in terms of Eurodollar
rates and the forward sterling discount (or premium). This
characteristic makes any attempt by the authorities to limit
residents' access to Eurosterling in isolation futile, because a
Eurodollar claim is a perfect substitute. Any control has to
extend to all currencies, as exchange controls did.

Table 7.2 gives details of the growth of the Eurosterling
market since 1976, based on data collected by the BIS.
Main centres of operation at March 1980 were Belgium—

Table 7.2 Eurosterling Assets and Liabilities (US $ bn)

End of Period	Banks' Liabilities	Banks' Claims	on which on London
1976	4.1	2.4	0.8
1977	6.0	4.7	2.2
1978	10.4	7.6	2.8
1979 March	12.2	8.6	2.6
June	13.2	8.6	2.7
September	15.0	9.8	3.3
December	15.3	11.6	5.4
1980 March	19.5	12.0	5.3

Source: Bank for International Settlements

Luxembourg ($5.6 bn), Netherlands ($5.0 bn) and France ($4.8 bn). Liabilities stood at $19.5 bn, and claims at $12.0 bn, of which nearly 45% were on UK residents (a quarter of these were 'working balances' held in London banks). These figures show the satellite character of the market, in terms of the extent to which deposits are switched into other currencies. They also show the rapid growth of the market in recent years including the one full quarter since exchange controls were abolished. None of the data are of the market free of restrictions, for UK banks were under voluntary restraint until the end of June 1980 not to use the Eurocurrency loophole.

That particular direction from the Governor is a clear admission that, in the new environment, controls cannot discriminate between domestic and external 'producers' of sterling intermediation. Banks could side-step the controls and avoid any tax by round-tripping customers' deposit and loan business through their overseas branches. Some of the growth since 1976 may be of domestic banking driven offshore by the corset. (Recently there has also been a revival of sterling as an internationally held currency).

American experience with the Eurodollar market is instructive. Because of the close links between domestic and 'Euro' interest rates (a theory of these links is developed in Johnston 1979), monetary restraint implemented either by means of interest rates or by increases in reserve requirements is quickly transmitted to the Eurodollar market, as it is to domestic parallel markets. Eurodollar rates rise in harmony with domestic interest rates, and monetary restraint is effective in this sense. But, as interest rates rise, intermediation in the Eurodollar market accelerates relative to domestic banking. US banks are required to hold non-interest bearing reserves and are prevented from paying interest on deposits of less than 30 days' maturity. Branches of the same banks in Europe are not similarly restrained, and business is shifted to them. Much the same story is true of German monetary policy because of the Euro-DM market in Luxembourg. Both authorities are unwilling to remove these restrictions because, in their judgment, they would be giving up important instruments which provide an 'effective', albeit partly cosmetic, control over the money supply without being sure about what would take their place. They also attempted, unsuccessfully, to persuade host countries to levy reserve requirements on Eurocurrency deposits. (This was in 1979.)

Following the abolition of the corset, the remaining British controls (Special Deposits, the cash requirement) do not impose a tax effect high enough to offset the additional costs of diverting business abroad (see Chapter 6). Whether monetary base control would stimulate a growth in Eurosterling business is more difficult to judge. To the extent that Eurobanks must themselves hold base money and reserves in order to provide for liquidity production, there seems little reason to expect it to do so. But if, as we have argued, wholesale banking can do without base money and domestic wholesale business is constrained by an imposed reserve ratio, it becomes a matter of whether the induced interest rate increases are sufficient to choke off any loan demands transferred to the Eurocentres.

Insofar as the authorities rely upon the interest rate weapon alone, the Eurosterling market does not pose a control problem, but it does give rise to an information problem. When deciding upon the level (or band) of interest rates, allowance needs to be made for Eurosterling deposits. In fact, residents' Eurosterling balances should perhaps be included in the definition of money. To do so, the quality of the data needs to be improved and the publication lag (currently about 4.5 months) reduced.

But the issues raised by the absence of exchange controls are more general when residents are free to hold foreign currency deposits. Not only is an £M3 definition suspect, but the money stock may not be capable of a satisfactory definition.[2] Suppose our objective is to have a monetary aggregate relevant to the financing of domestic expenditure decisions. Eurosterling balances of residents, we have suggested, seem relevant. But these balances, or borrowings, can be spent anywhere in the world, not just in Britain. Balances held by residents in foreign currencies may be primarily for foreign trade, but some part is likely to stimulate spending in the UK. For example, a firm building a new plant in the UK with imported equipment, and for which production is to be exported, might avert exchange risks by dealing in one of the major vehicle currencies. Then there is the question of the domestic deposits of non-residents. Imagine the consequences of trying to define the money supply relevant to Scotland. Would we include 'Scottish' deposits held with banks in England? How would we treat 'English' deposits with banks in Scotland? Would only Scottish note issue be included? A large amount of 'foreign' deposits and 'foreign' assets may govern expenditure decisions in Scotland.

For most countries, the issues posed by currency diversification are a problem for the future. In the case of Britain, they could be more immediate. It used to be said that exchange control and Euromarkets went hand in hand. For example:

> Countries with convertible currencies and active Eurocurrency markets, such as Belgium, France, Italy, and Japan, often insulate the purely domestic portion of their banking system by a web of exchange controls on capital-account transactions similar to the British. The logic here is straightforward. If there are no controls on capital-account transfers into foreign monies by domestic residents, the authorities tend to regulate foreign-currency deposits more severely to prevent a decline in the use of the domestic currency as domestic money. Among major countries, Britain seems to grant the greatest regulatory freedom to commercial banks accepting deposits and loans in foreign currencies. Consequently, Britain has the greatest need to protect the domain of sterling with exchange controls. (McKinnon 1977)

Britain is putting that view to the test. It is now unique in the world as a country which simultaneously has no exchange control but also exempts domestic banks from reserve requirements on foreign currency business (Llewellyn 1979b).

Britain has been led to this position by the short run exigencies of the strength of sterling in 1979 and the longer run appeal of a free market solution — the financial analogue of free trade in commodities. In it, borrowers choose a preferred portfolio of currencies and national securities, lenders obtain funds from the cheapest sources, while intermediaries locate production where costs are lowest. But there is an obvious difficulty if national authorities allow the market to choose its preferred position and then adapt their control mechanisms to that choice. Efficiency gains do not stop at national boundaries. For private transactors, the optimum size of the integrated area is the world! Flexible exchange rates are no help, for these render currencies less perfect substitutes in terms of their supply, but not necessarily in demand. Indeed, by making national currencies less good substitutes for the principal vehicle currencies (which could include sterling), they raise the returns to be had from currency diversification (Miles 1978).

So far their new-found freedom has not led UK residents to change the relationship between £M3 and M3 (which includes some of the non-sterling deposits which residents are free to hold). We have deliberately overstated the present dangers to make the point that as financial integration grows and currency diversification of money holdings increases, the potential exists for a severe loss of monetary autonomy. Control of the volume of liquid assets denominated in a particular currency (even if possible with Euromarkets) has less and less leverage over macroeconomic conditions in that country. The money supply which is relevant for domestic spending includes monies of other countries. In the limit, monetary policies become meaningless at the national level and must be conducted at a global level by control of the 'world' money supply. For individual countries, a greater influence upon internal financial conditions could come from exchange rate management. (That, at least, is the view of Williamson 1980.)

Part of the thrust of the idea of the European Monetary System (EMS) is to form an aggregation of countries, already closely linked, in which such a global approach to monetary policy could eventually work. We now comment upon British participation in it.

Membership of EMS and Exchange Rate Policies

Britain already participates in some aspects of EMS. By 'joining EMS' we mean adherence to the intervention principles by which exchange rate movements are stabilised between member states of the EEC. Like the old 'snake', these band arrangements are a first step towards eventual monetary union in the Community. EMS works as follows:

(a) For each currency in the system, a central rate is fixed in ECUs (European Currency Units) which is a monetary unit based on a basket of member currencies. Sterling has a 13.3% weight. The central rate can be modified, subject to mutual agreement, to take account of changed circumstances. EMS thus implies fixed, but adjustable, exchange rates between the EEC currencies.

(b) These central rates are used to establish a grid of bilateral exchange rates. Around these rates fluctuation margins have been established: for most countries the maximum margin is 2.25%, but a wider margin up to 6% can be adopted (so far only by Italy).

(c) Obligatory market intervention points are fixed. Central banks in the participating countries are obliged to intervene to keep their exchange rate within the agreed margins.

(d) Participants place 20% of their gold and dollar reserves in a Co-operation Fund and receive a supply of ECUs and credit mechanisms to regulate intervention. These support facilities are designed to dissuade speculators and thereby alleviate the monetary risks to member states.

Britain participates in the credit mechanism, but so far is the only member state not involved in the more important exchange rate provisions. These arrangements were agreed to in December 1978 and have been in force since March 1979.

Should Britain join, some limitation would be implied

upon the range over which the effective rate of sterling could vary, relative to that experienced recently. Although sterling would remain floating against other countries (unless EMS members adopted a common dollar strategy), participation means observing prescribed margins for sterling against EMS currencies. At the same time membership would be meaningless if the parity changed every time sterling pushed against the intervention limits. It follows that to avoid parity changes, other arms of domestic policy would have to be supportive.

Monetary policy, then, would not be redundant but its role would be altered. Its job would be to ensure that the exchange rate target is met. A target for the rate of monetary growth, or for DCE, consistent with the exchange rate grid could always be declared, based on macroeconomic forecasts of behavioural relationships and exogenous factors such as oil prices. Inconsistencies between the two would arise in practice. Then one of the targets would have to give way, presumably the monetary target.

This illustrates that, in the context of EMS membership, monetary targets are subordinate to exchange rate targets. If the UK did not join the system, or became a full member only on the basis of being able to exploit a much larger degree of exchange rate flexibility than seems compatible with the long run aims of the system, then there would be an opportunity to adopt a compromise regime in which the monetary target would be conditionalised on the behaviour of the exchange rate.

There are at least two principal lines of argument which suggest that, in one way or another, monetary targets are likely to be more or less diluted by consideration for exchange rate developments. First, there is the problem of dynamic adjustment of the exchange rate to programmes of monetary growth control in which it has become clear (Dornbusch 1980, Buiter and Miller 1981) that the exchange rate has a strong propensity to 'overshoot', with consequent excessive unemployment and recession. Second, even if we accept the primacy of the anti-inflation goal of policy, monetary targets are not the only means of achieving this end. It is true that some fixed point is needed if nominal magnitudes in the economic system are to be determined. In the context of general equilibrium models the role of determining absolute prices from a set of relative prices is usually given to the quantity of money. But there is no formal reason why the general price level could not be determined by fixing the price for some important specific good such as labour, by an incomes policy, or by fixing the price of foreign exchange, by an EMS-type arrangement.

An exchange rate target has appeal for those who regard inflation and incomes in Britain as generated mainly by external factors. But if inflation has domestic origins, an exchange rate policy could still bring benefits. Indeed, it can be argued that the transmission from money to output and prices works largely through the effect upon the exchange rate and that to set a target for the exchange rate neatly encapsulates the main rationale for setting a target for money. Of course, the value of a particular target cannot be judged without reference to the precision and efficacy of the instruments which are available, or likely to be used, to achieve it. Views about the controllability of a monetary *vis-à-vis* an exchange rate target may have undergone some transformation since 1979.

There is then the question of whether an exchange rate commitment arising from EMS membership would have the same leverage upon expectations of inflation as the current process of setting (if not exactly achieving) monetary targets. In some eyes the impact upon public perceptions could be aided. Governments in the EMS countries have been equally unequivocal in declaring a reduction of inflation to be the major policy objective, and with the Deutsche Mark having a weight of 33% in the ECU, German monetary policy seems likely to be the dominant influence upon common inflationary pressures. Sumner and Zis (1981) argue that the transition to lower inflation after 1979 would have been achieved more efficaciously had Britain joined EMS and not gone it alone with monetary targets. They find it difficult to believe that a higher inflation rate would have been expected by the British public. At the same time, British industry might have been spared such a large real appreciation of the pound with its adverse impact upon the 'supply side' of the economy.

Nevertheless, it must be said that purely from the point of view of inflation control, the EMS provides a much less than ideal setting for exchange rate targeting, for at least two reasons. First, as far as the UK is concerned, it is important to note that this country continues to conduct a large proportion (much higher than that of other system members) of its trade with non-EMS member countries; this considerably dilutes the relevance of a fixed parity *vis-à-vis* EMS members. Second, if the control of inflation is important, it is presumably absolute and not relative inflation (relative to other countries, that is) which counts; but if so, the ideal form of exchange rate targeting will be some form of 'gliding parity' rather than a fixed (if adjustable) peg of the EMS type.

While Britain might have joined EMS, and may even join now, at a parity consistent with its chosen monetary and inflation objectives, her freedom to choose the stance of monetary policy would diminish as the parity is sustained. Over time, the rate of inflation and the level of interest rates would be governed by those of the policies of EMS members as a whole. It becomes a question of whether the UK is prepared to make this economic, and ultimately, political, commitment to the EEC.

Here we are led back to the issues of monetary autonomy raised more generally by financial integration in a post exchange control world, for Britain may be unable in the longer run to retain her scope for monetary independence along with adherence to market-based solutions. Amongst the European partners, there may be a recognition that the Eurocurrency markets are producing a degree of financial integration such that a global approach to monetary matters is beginning to make sense anyway — in which case, they prefer the global solution to be a European one, than to be some other.

Notes to Chapter 7

1 Williamson (1980) notes that those previously denied the opportunity to speculate could have judgments similar to those of the authorities and be a new counteracting source of stabilising speculation in the foreign exchange market.
2 Alternatively, if the money stock is defined as before, its velocity may exhibit high elasticity with respect to 'foreign' interest rates.

Bibliography

Akerlof, G.A. & Milbourne, R.D. (1980), The short run demand for money, *Economic Journal*, Vol. 90, pp. 885–900.

Artis, M.J. (1978), Monetary policy – Part II, in F.T. Blackaby (ed.), *British Economic Policy 1960–1974*, Cambridge University Press.

Artis, M.J. & Currie, D.A. (1981), Monetary and exchange rate targets, in A.S. Courakis and R.L. Harrington (eds), *Monetarism: Traditions, Theory and Policy*, Macmillan.

Artis, M.J. & Lewis, M.K. (1974), The demand for money: stable or unstable?, *The Banker*, Vol. 124, pp. 239–47.

Artis, M.J. & Lewis, M.K. (1976), The demand for money in the UK, 1963–1973, *Manchester School*, Vol. 44, pp. 147–81.

Artis, M.J. & Nobay, R.A. (1969), Two aspects of the monetary debate, *National Institute Economic Review*, No. 49, August.

Baltensperger, E. (1980), Alternative approaches to the theory of the banking firm, *Journal of Monetary Economics*, pp. 1–37.

Bank of England (1968), Overseas and foreign banks in London 1962–1968, *Bank of England Quarterly Bulletin*, June.

Bank of England (1971a), Monetary management in the UK, *Bank of England Quarterly Bulletin*, March.

Bank of England (1971b), Competition and credit control, *Bank of England Quarterly Bulletin*, December.

Bank of England (1974), Competition and credit control. Articles from the *Bank of England Quarterly Bulletin*, 1971–74.

Bank of England (1978), Reflections on the conduct of monetary policy, *Bank of England Quarterly Bulletin*, March.

Bank of England (1981), The UK corporate bond market, *Bank of England Quarterly Bulletin*, March.

Baumol, W.J. (1952), The transactions demand for cash: an inventory theoretic approach, *Quarterly Journal of Economics*, 66, pp. 545–56.

Benston, G.J. & Smith, C.W. (1976), A transactions cost approach to the theory of financial intermediation, *Journal of Finance*, pp. 215–31.

Bladen-Hovell, R., Green, C & Savage, D. (1981), The monetary transmission mechanism in the Treasury and National Institute models, *Manchester University Discussion Paper Series*.

Blanden, M. (1980), How the Bank's liquidity controls will bite, *The Banker*, vol. 130, July, pp. 25–8.

Blunden, G. (1975), The supervision of the UK banking system, *Bank of England Quarterly Bulletin*, June.

Boughton, J.M. (1979), Demand for money in major OECD countries, *OECD Economic Outlook Occasional Studies*, January.

Brunner, K. & Meltzer, A.H. (1964), *An Alternative Approach to the Monetary Mechanism*, Sub-Committee on Domestic Finance, Committee on Banking and Currency, US Government Printing Office, Washington DC.

Buiter, W. & Miller, M.H. (1981), Monetary policy and international competitiveness, *Oxford Economic Papers*, July.

Coghlan, R.T. (1977), Analysis within the 'new view', *Journal of Money, Credit and Banking*, Vol. 9, pp. 410–27.

Coghlan, R.T. (1978a), A transactions demand for money, *Bank of England Quarterly Bulletin*, March, pp. 48–60.

Coghlan, R.T. (1978b), A new view of money, *Lloyds Bank Review*, No. 129, pp. 12–27.

Coghlan, R.T. (1979), A small monetary model of the UK economy, *Bank of England Discussion Paper*, No. 3.

Coghlan, R.T. (1980a), *The Theory of Money and Finance*, Macmillan.

Coghlan, R.T. (1980b), The role of domestic credit expansion in money supply, *The Banker*, January, pp. 45–8.

Coghlan R.T. & Sykes, C. (1980), Managing the money supply, *Lloyds Bank Review*, No. 135, pp. 1–13.

Congdon, T.G. (1980a), Should Britain adopt monetary base control?, *The Banker*, February.

Congdon, T.G. (1980b), The monetary base debate: another instalment in the currency school vs. banking school controversy, *National Westminster Bank Quarterly Review*, August, pp. 2–13.

Congdon, T.G. (1980c), The lender of last resort function: its role in monetary control, *L. Messel and Co. Newsletter*, 24 October.

Courakis, A.S. (1978), Serial correlation and a Bank of England study of the demand for money: an exercise in measurement without theory, *Economic Journal*, Vol. 88, pp. 537–48.

Davis, K.T. & Lewis, M.K. (1980), *Monetary Policy in Australia*, Longmans, Melbourne.

Davis, K.T. & Lewis, M.K. (1981), Foreign banks and the financial system, in *Australian Financial System Inquiry, Commissioned Studies and Selected Papers*, Vol. 1, Australian Government Publishing Service, Canberra.

Dornbusch, R. (1980), *Open Economy Macroeconomics*, Basic Books, New York.

Dow, J.C.R. (1958), The economic effect of monetary policy 1945–57, Committee on the Working of the Monetary System, *Principal Memoranda of Evidence*, Vol. 3, HMSO 1960, pp. 76–105.

Duck, N.W. & Sheppard, D.K. (1978), A proposal for the control of the UK money supply, *Economic Journal*, Vol. 88, pp. 1–17.

Federal Reserve Bank of New York (1980), Financial innovations in Canada, *Federal Reserve Bank of New York Quarterly Review*, Autumn.

Fisher, D. (1968), The demand for money in Britain: quarterly results 1951 to 1967, *The Manchester School*, Vol. 36, pp. 239–344.

Foot, M.D.K.W. (1981), Monetary targets: their nature and record in the major economies, in B. Griffiths and G.E. Wood (eds), *Monetary Targets*, Macmillan, (forthcoming).

Foot, M.D.K.W., Goodhart, C.A.E. & Hotson, A.C. (1979), Monetary base control, *Bank of England Quarterly Bulletin*, pp. 149–59.

Freedman, C.W. (1977), Microtheory of international financial intermediation, *American Economic Review* 67, pp. 172–79.

Friedman, M. (1956), The quantity theory of money – a restatement, in M. Friedman (ed.), *Studies in the Quantity Theory of Money*, Chicago University Press.

Friedman, M. (1972), Monetary trends in the United States and the United Kingdom, *American Economist*, Vol. 16, pp. 4–17.

Friedman, M. (1977), Nobel lecture: inflation and unemployment, *Journal of Political Economy*, June.

Friedman, M. (1980a), Prices of money and goods across frontiers: the £ and $ over a century, *World Economy*, Vol. 2, pp. 497–511.

Friedman, M. (1980b), Memorandum on monetary policy in Treasury and Civil Service Committee, *Memoranda on Monetary Policy*, Series 1979–80, HMSO.

Goodhart, C.A.E. (1973), Alternatives for debt management: discussion, in Federal Reserve Bank of Boston, *Issues in Federal Debt Management*, Conference Series No. 10.

Goodhart, C.A.E. (1978), Money in an open economy, Conference on Economic Modelling, *London Business School*.

Goodhart, C.A.E. (1979), Problems of monetary management: the UK experience, in A.S. Courakis (ed.), *Inflation, Depression and Economic Policy in the West: lessons from the 1970s*, Mansell and Alexandrine Press.

Goodhart, C.A.E. & Crockett, A.D. (1970), The importance of money, *Bank of England Quarterly Bulletin*, June, pp. 159–98.

Gowland, D. (1978), *Monetary Policy and Credit Control*, Croom Helm.

Griffiths, B. (1979), The reform of monetary control in the United Kingdom, *Annual Monetary Review*, No. 1, pp. 29–41.

Griffiths, B. (1980), Has the Green Paper got it wrong?, *The Times*, 6th May.

Hacche, G.J. (1974), The demand for money in the United Kingdom: experience since 1971, *Bank of England Quarterly Bulletin*, September, pp. 284–305.

Hahn, F. (1980), Submission on monetary policy in Treasury and Civil Service Committee, *Memoranda on Monetary Policy*, Series 1979–1980, HMSO.

Hamburger, M.J. (1977), The demand for money in an open economy, Germany and the United Kingdom, *Journal of Monetary Economics*, Vol. 3, pp. 25–40.

Harrod, R.F. (1969), *Money*, Macmillan.

Hendry, D.F. & Mizon, G.E. (1978), Serial correlation as a convenient simplification, not as a nuisance: a comment on a study of the demand for money by the Bank of England, *Economic Journal*, Vol. 88.

Herring, R.J. & Marston, R.C. (1978), *National Monetary Policies and International Financial Markets*, North-Holland Publishing Co.

Hewson, J. (1975), *Liquidity Creation and Distribution in the Euro-Currency Markets*, Lexington Books, Mass.

Hilliard, B.C. (1980), The Bank of England small monetary model: recent developments and simulation properties, *Bank of England Discussion Paper*, No. 13.

Hoffman, J.M. (1980), A quarterly small monetary model of the UK economy: preliminary estimation and simulation results, *Bank of England Discussion Paper*, No. 14.

Hotson, A.C. (1979), The forecasting and control of bank lending. Paper presented at *Money Study Group Conference on Monetarism*, Oxford, September.

Johnson, C. (1980a), The meaning of money, *Lloyds Bank Economic Bulletin*, No. 13, January.

Johnson, C. (1980b), A monetarist strategy, *Lloyds Bank Economic Bulletin*, No. 17, May.

Johnson, C. (1980c), Industry may borrow less, *Lloyds Bank Economic Bulletin*, No. 23, November.

Johnson, H.G. (1972), *Further Essays in Monetary Economics*, Allen & Unwin.

Johnston, R.B. (1979), Some aspects of the determination of euro-currency interest rates, *Bank of England Quarterly Bulletin*, Vol. 19, pp. 35–46.

Jonson, P.D. (1976), Money, prices and output: an integrative essay, *Kredit Kapital*, 4th Quarter.

Jonson, P.D., Moses, E.R. & Wymer, C.R. (1976), A minimal model of the Australian economy, *Reserve Bank of Australia, Research Discussion Paper* 7601, reprinted in W.E. Norton (ed.), *Conference in Applied Economic Research*, Reserve Bank of Australia, Sydney, 1977.

Kaldor, N.C. (1970), The new monetarism, *Lloyds Bank Review*, April.

Kavanagh, N.J. & Walters, A.A. (1966), The demand for money in the

United Kingdom, 1877–1961, *Bulletin of the Oxford University Institute of Economics and Statistics*, Vol. 28, pp. 93–116.

Keynes, J.M. (1936), *The General Theory of Employment, Interest and Money*, Macmillan.

Klein, M.A. (1971), A theory of the banking firm, *Journal of Money, Credit and Banking*, May, 205–18.

Laidler, D.E.W. (1971), The influence of money on economic activity – a survey of some current problems, in G. Clayton, J.C. Gilbert and R. Sedgwick (eds), *Monetary Theory and Monetary Policy in the 1970s*, Oxford University Press.

Laidler, D.E.W. (1973), Monetarist policy prescriptions and their background, *Manchester School*, Vol. 41, pp. 59–71.

Laidler, D.E.W. (1977), *The Demand for Money*, 2nd edition, Dun-Donelley, New York.

Laidler, D.E.W. & Parkin, J.M. (1970), The demand for money in the United Kingdom, 1955–1967: preliminary estimates, *The Manchester School*, Vol. 38, pp. 187–208.

Lewis, M.K. (1978), Interest rates and monetary velocity in Australia and the United States, *Economic Record*, Vol. 54, pp. 111–26.

Lewis, M.K. (1980a), Are banks controlled because they are different or different because they are controlled?, *Economic Papers*, No. 63, pp. 25–40.

Lewis, M.K. (1980b), Rethinking monetary policy, *Lloyds Bank Review* No. 137, July, pp. 41–60.

Lewis, M.K. (1980c), Is monetary base control just interest rate control in disguise?, *The Banker*, Vol. 130, pp. 35–8.

Lewis, M.K. (1981), Monetarism in Australia: a test case for British policies?, in A.S. Courakis and R.L. Harrington (eds), *Monetarism: Traditions, Theory and Policy*, Macmillan.

Lindbeck, A. (1978), Economic dependence and interdependence in the industrialized world, in *From Marshall Plan to Global Interdependence*, OECD, Paris.

Lipsey, R.G. & Parkin, J.M. (1970), Incomes policy: re re-appraisal, *Economica* (NS), Vol. 37, pp. 115–38.

Llewellyn, D.T. (1979a), Do building societies take deposits away from banks? *Lloyds Bank Review*, No. 131, pp. 21–34.

Llewellyn, D.T. (1979b), End of the UK exchange control: the monetary implications, *The Banker*, December, pp. 43–7.

Lomax, D.F. (1980), Monetary policy, *National Westminster Bank Quarterly Review*, November.

Lucas, R.E. & Sargent, T.J. (1979), After Keynesian macroeconomics, *Federal Reserve Bank of Minneapolis Quarterly Review*, Spring, pp. 1–16.

McKinnon, R.I. (1977), The eurocurrency market, *Essays in International Finance*, No. 125, Princeton.

McMahon, C.W. (1981), The financial scene in the 1970s, *Bank of England Quarterly Bulletin*, Vol. 21, March, pp. 71–6.

Mangoletsis, I.D. (1975), The micro-economics of indirect finance, *Journal of Finance*, September, pp. 1055–63.

Miles, M.A. (1978), Currency substitution, flexible exchange rates, and monetary independence, *American Economic Review*, Vol. 68, pp. 428—36.

Mills, T.C. (1978a), The functional form of the UK demand for money, *Journal of the Royal Statistical Society*, Series C, Vol. 27, pp 52—7.

Mills, T.C. (1978b), Money, income and causality in the UK — a look at the recent experience, *University of Leeds Discussion Paper Series*, May.

Mills, T.C. & Wood, G.E. (1978), Money — income relationships and the exchange, *Federal Reserve Bank of St. Louis Review*, Vol. 60, No. 8, August, pp. 22—7.

Moore, B.J. & Threadgold, A.R. (1980), Bank lending and the money supply, *Bank of England Discussion Paper*, No. 10.

Niehans, J. (1978), *The theory of money*, John Hopkins, Baltimore.

Niehans, J. & Hewson, J. (1976), The euro-dollar market and monetary theory, *Journal of Money, Credit and Banking*, February, pp. 1—28.

Paish, F.W. (1958), The future of British monetary policy, Committee on the Working of the Monetary System, *Principal Memoranda of Evidence*, Vol 3, HMSO 1960, pp. 182—8.

Paish, F.W. (1959), Gilt-edged and the money supply, *The Banker*, Vol. 109, January.

Patinkin, D. (1965), *Money, Interest and Prices: An Integration of Monetary and Value Theory*, 2nd edition, Harper and Row, New York.

Pepper, G. (1979), Monetary control in the UK. Talk to Institute of Bankers, London, W. Greenwell & Co., *Monetary Bulletin*, October.

Poole, W. (1970), Optimal choice of monetary policy instruments in a simple stochastic macro model, *Quarterly Journal of Economics*, Vol. 84, pp. 197—216.

Price, L.D.D. (1972), The demand for money in the United Kingdom: a further investigation, *Bank of England Quarterly Bulletin*, Vol. 12, March.

Pyle, D.H. (1971), On the theory of financial intermediation, *Journal of Finance*, June, pp. 737—47.

Revell, J. (1968), A secondary banking system, *The Banker*, Vol. 118, September.

Revell, J. (1975), Solvency and regulation of banks, *Bangor Occasional Papers in Economics*, 5.

Revell, J. (1978), Competition and regulation of banks, *Bangor Occasional Papers in Economics*, 14.

Revell, J. (1980), *Costs and Margins in Banking: An International Survey*, OECD, Paris.

Robertson, D.H. (1922), *Money*, Cambridge Economic Handbook.

Rowan, D.C. & Miller, J. (1979), The demand for money in the United Kingdom 1963—1977, *Southampton University Discussion Paper in Economics and Econometrics*, 7902.

Savage, D. (1978), The channels of monetary influence: a survey of the empirical evidence, *National Institute Economic Review*, No. 83, February, pp. 73—89.

Savage, D. (1980), Some issues of monetary policy, *National Institute Economic Review*, No. 91, February, pp. 78—85.

Saving, T.R. (1977), A theory of money supply with competitive banking, *Journal of Monetary Economics*, July, pp. 289—303.

Sealey, C.W. & Lindley, J.T. (1977), Inputs, outputs and a theory of production and cost at depository financial institutions, *Journal of Finance*, September, pp. 1251—66.

Smith, D. (1978), The demand for alternative monies in the UK: 1924—1977, *National Westminster Bank Quarterly Review*, November, pp. 35—49.

Sumner, M. & Zis, G. (1981), Whither European monetary union?, *National Westminster Bank Quarterly Review*, February, pp. 49—61.

Taylor, C.T. & Threadgold, A.R. (1979), 'Real' national saving and its sectoral composition, *Bank of England Discussion Paper*, No. 6.

Tew, J.H.B., (1978), Monetary policy — part 1, in F.T. Blackaby (ed.), *British Economic Policy 1960—1974*, Cambridge University Press, pp. 218—57.

Tew, J.H.B. (1981), The implementation of monetary policy in post-war Britain, *Midland Bank Review*, Spring, pp. 5—14.

Tobin, J. (1956), The interest-elasticity of transactions demand for cash, *Review of Economics and Statistics*, Vol. 38, pp. 241—7.

Tobin, J. (1958), Liquidity preference as behaviour towards risk, *Review of Economic Studies*, Vol. 25, pp. 65—86.

Towey, R.E. (1974), Money creation and the theory of the banking firm, *Journal of Finance*, March, 57—72.

Weston, C.R. (1980), *Domestic and Multinational Banking*, Croom Helm.

Williams, D., Goodhart, C.A.E. & Gowland, D.H. (1976), Money, income and causality: the UK experience, *American Economic Review*, June, Vol. 66.

Williamson, J. (1980), Response to questionnaire on monetary policy in Treasury and Civil Service Committee, *Memoranda on Monetary Policy, Series 1979—80*, HMSO, London.

Wood, G.E. (1979), Cash base control of the money supply — its institutional implications, *The Banker*, July, pp. 37—43.

Wood, P. (1980), Reform need not be so complex, *Euromoney*, June, pp. 65—76.

Index

Accepting houses, 3, 6, 86—7
Advances, 83, 117, 134
  interest rates on, 36, 83
  requests, 2, 8, 24
Aggregate demand, 41

Balance of payments, 38, 41—2, 50,
  59, 72—3
  capital account, 71, 73, 140 (see
  also Capital flows)
  current account, 54, 71, 73
  and monetary policy, 11
Bank reserve,
  assets ratio, 1, 7—8, 63, 73, 76,
  85, 104, 139
  requirements, 31, 34, 71, 108—10,
  130, 139, 141
Banking Act, (The Act), 1, 9, 104, 118
Base money, 122—9, 131, 139
Bills, 3, 7, 13, 40—1, 64—5, 88, 114,
  119, 122—3
  Treasury_ , 9, 34, 40, 64—5, 71,
  76, 80, 112
Bonds, 7, 13—14, 16, 22, 31, 36, 44,
  67, 78, 119, 122—3, 133
Building societies, 39, 49, 51, 59, 93,
  104, 115, 118, 135

Cambridge 'K', 13, 27 (see also
  Velocity)
Capital, 75, 91—2, 110
  real cost of, 49
Capital of banks,
  adequacy, 1, 103
  funds, 70
  measurement of, 10, 102, 105
  reserves, 70
Capital flows, 49—50, 52, 73
  inflows, 36
  outflows, 52, 56
  short term, 54
Cash, 64—6, 81, 85, 92—3, 97, 106—7,
  122—3, 125, 130, 139
  ratio, 64, 85, 111—12
  reserve, 3, 7—8, 112, 122
Cheque paying banks, 3
Clearing banks, 2, 3, 7, 26, 33, 48, 58,
  61, 64—5, 80, 86—90, 96, 101, 103,
  111—12, 117, 120, 135
  cartel arrangements, 5, 7, 14, 23

Competition and Credit Control, 2, 6—
  10, 14, 17, 22—3, 25, 29, 31—3, 36,
  38, 43, 65, 92, 96, 103, 110
Consols,
  rate, 27, 29
  yields on, 13, 26
Consumption, 49—51
Cooperation Fund, 142
Credit, 68, 83, 90, 113, 119, 122—4,
  128, 134
  allocation, 9
  conditions, 8, 62, 114
  control, 2, 6—7, 9—10, 17, 22, 24,
  104, 113, 117
  counterparts, 73, 84, 86
  creation, 8, 63, 93
  interest elasticity of, 84
  restriction_ , 14
Crowding out, 74
Currency, 3, 14, 26, 58, 64, 66—7, 71,
  85, 88, 90, 92, 96—8, 102, 105,
  125, 127, 136, 140—41

Demand management, 42—3
Demand for money, 6—9, 11—14, 16,
  17, 23—5, 32—4, 38, 39, 46, 48,
  50, 54, 61, 62, 75, 123
  income elasticity of, 12—15, 17, 20,
  24, 26, 29, 32, 38
  interest elasticity of, 11—13, 15,
  17, 20, 27, 29, 32, 36, 56
  long run_ , 14—15, 20, 24—5, 29, 37
  price elasticity of, 12—13
  short run_ , 6, 12, 15—17, 33, 55
  stable (stability of), 6, 9, 11, 15,
  17, 20, 22, 24—6, 29, 32, 37, 55,
  62
  theories of, 12
  transactions motive, 12, 20, 75
  wealth effects, 12, 75
Deposit, 3, 23, 30, 63, 67, 70—73, 76,
  81, 86, 88, 90—94, 96—7, 101,
  104—7, 110, 116, 120—23, 125,
  134, 136—7, 138, 140
  bank_ , 13, 30, 33—4, 51, 61, 72,
  76, 84, 86, 93, 114, 125
  _banks, 3, 33, 86, 90, 96, 115—20,
  127, 129
  Certificates of (CD), 23, 30, 34,
  113, 115, 119

in clearing banks, 14, 48, 58, 88
foreign currency_ , 58, 67, 71–2,
136–7, 140
interest bearing_ ,22–3, 30, 33,
112–3
_ rates, 3, 23, 33–4, 36, 61, 84,
112, 114–5, 122
short term_ , 64, 135
sight_ , 22, 59, 90
special_ , 7, 9, 40, 63, 73, 85, 108,
110–12, 128–9, 131, 139
_ taking institutions, 1, 9, 104
time_ , 22, 33–4, 56, 59, 106, 120
Discount,
houses, 3, 33, 40, 64–5, 89
markets, 62–5
window, 129
Dollar,
reserves, 142
strategy, 143
Domestic credit expansion (DCE),
38–9, 50–1, 54–5, 57, 68, 71,
73, 143

Eligible liabilities (EL's), 73, 85,
112–13, 135
Employment, 40, 42–4, 60, 75, 84,
133, 143
Euro,
bank, 137, 139
banking system, 88
centres, 88, 139
currency, 98, 107, 137–40, 145
DM, 139
dollar, 34, 137–9
interest rates, 138
markets, 9, 58, 88, 90, 105, 140–1,
sterling, 85, 113–4, 127, 137,
139–40
European Currency Units, 142, 144
European Monetary System, 132,
141–5
Exchanges,
controls, 1, 9, 16, 52, 58, 71,
88, 105, 109, 136–8, 140, 145
market, 54
Exchange rate, 43, 49, 51–4, 58, 68,
70–1, 73, 105, 125, 132–3, 136,
142–5
fixed, 11, 16, 38, 42–3, 50
flexible (floating), 11, 24, 42,
48, 50, 52, 72–3, 141

Finance houses, 2, 7, 64, 115
Financial institutions (intermediaries),

3, 7, 40, 91, 95, 102, 110, 115
integration of, 132, 141, 145
Financial market (sector, system), 1,
40, 59, 61, 83, 86, 104, 114–15
competition in, 2, 17
Fiscal,
deficit, 24, 31, 54, 74
policy, 9, 58, 68, 70, 73–4, 84,
124, 133

Gilt(s), 34, 68, 71, 75–6, 78, 84
Gilted-edged,
markets, 24, 62, 74–5, 82
rates, 27
securities, 36, 40, 78
Gold reserves, 142

High-powered money, 92, 127–9

Incomes policy, 42, 144
Inflation, 11–12, 40–1, 44, 46, 48–
9, 51, 53, 60, 78, 81, 132–3, 135,
143–5
expected (expectations of), 12, 29,
41–3, 49, 51, 53–4, 78
Interbank,
borrowings, 122, 124
deposits, 88, 106
funds, 101
market, 65, 93, 101, 103, 106,
117–19, 123, 129
rate, 33, 119, 123
settlements, 92
standby facilities, 106
transactions, 106
Interest rate(s),
and borrowing, 80
ceilings, 3, 8, 121
control, 8, 10, 108, 110, 115, 121,
124, 129
on credit and bank lending, 80–81
long term, 22, 34
market, 14, 33, 36, 61
as a market instrument, 7–8, 11,
36, 95
monetary policy effect on _, 11
on money (own rate of interest), 12,
14, 22, 23, 29, 31, 56
nominal, 13, 22, 41–2, 72, 82
real, 41, 42, 82
_ regulations, 2
short term, 10, 22, 41, 65, 78
structure of, 24, 62, 64–5, 96, 100,
109
_ and supply of money, 7, 25, 49, 66

Intermediation, 8, 10, 17, 23, 31, 83,
    85–6, 92, 94, 100, 104, 109–11,
    114, 119–20, 124, 129, 138–9
International Monetary Fund, 38–9, 52
Investment, 42–3, 49–50
IS, 11, 49, 50

Keynesian, 74
    interventions, 44
    liquidity preference, 27

Last resort,
    facilities, 63
    funds, 125
    loans, 65, 106
Lending, 66–8, 72, 76, 88, 96, 124,
    129, 131, 137
    bank_, 39, 41, 48–9, 54, 58, 61,
    67, 71, 78–85, 112–13, 117, 119,
    132–6
    control over, 2, 24
    directives, 2
    rates, 23, 85, 118, 133
Liquidity, 1, 9, 26, 34, 50–51, 63, 75,
    91–2, 94, 96, 100, 103–6, 112,
    119, 122, 124, 127, 136, 139
    assets ratio, 3, 7, 90
    'general', 8, 22
    'the measurement of', 10, 102
    _ preference, 27, 36, 77
    prudential_, 9
    PSL1, 9, 57
    PSL2, 9, 57, 59, 135
LM, 11, 36, 48, 50
Loan(s), 6, 65, 81–2, 90–91, 94,
    100–101, 103, 105–6, 112, 117–
    20, 134–5, 138–40
    rates, 24, 81, 110, 118, 120, 122–3,
    133
Loanable funds, 27, 75, 77
Local authority, 33, 64
    borrowing rates, 13
Lorenz curves, 97

Minimum Lending Rate (MLR, Bank
    rate), 2–3, 34, 41, 63–5, 80, 83,
    115, 117
Monetarists (monetarism), 6, 11, 36,
    38, 44, 48, 50, 54, 84
Monetary,
    affairs (matters), 114–45
    aggregates, 6–7, 9, 38–9, 40–42,
    44, 46, 48, 51, 73, 77, 140
    authorities, 6
    changes, 45

    conditions, 8
    constraint (restriction), 10, 34, 138
    control(s), 1, 2, 7, 9, 31–4, 37, 59,
    61, 68, 70, 73, 75, 77, 84–6, 88,
    90, 94, 102, 104–5, 107–8, 121,
    123, 130, 132–3
    creation, 54
    deviation, 136
    disequilibrium, 34, 37, 39, 50, 56,
    62
    disturbance, 70, 94
    expansion, 73
    forces, 48
    growth, 34, 39, 43, 48, 51–2, 60–
    61, 70, 72–3, 81, 117, 121, 123–4,
    132, 143
    independence (autonomy), 141, 145
    influences, 49
    instruments, 9, 63, 73
    management, 10, 44
    objectives, 65, 70, 73, 145
    risks, 142
    rule, 42
    shocks, 48
    strategy (see Monetary policy)
    targets, 44, 51–5, 62, 73–5, 80,
    82, 88, 108, 130, 135–6, 143–4
    theory, 50, 59
    units, 142
Monetary base control, 1, 10, 58, 84–
    5, 107–108, 110, 121–31, 134, 139
Monetary policy, 1, 2, 3, 6, 11, 17, 36,
    38, 40, 42, 45, 49, 51, 56, 59–61,
    82, 110, 114, 117–19, 123, 141–5
    and direct controls, 2, 6–8, 109–
    114, 117, 121
    German_, 139
    goal variables of, 40, 44–5, 51, 55,
    58–9
    instrument variables of, 40, 45
    intermediate variables of, 40, 45, 52
Money,
    as abode of purchasing power, 16,
    36–7, 93, 120
    base_, 92–3, 96, 122–5, 127–8,
    131, 139
    as a buffer stock, 16, 50
    call_, 7
    definition of, 17, 26, 66–73, 139
    demand determined, 14, 16, 17, 23,
    32, 46, 55
    domestic, 43
    foreign, 43
    high-powered, 92
    illusion, 13

to income ratio, 13–15, 26–7, 32
interest bearing, 90
market, 10, 23, 24, 32, 39, 49, 62, 73, 82, 88, 93, 94, 113, 114, 135
M1, 6, 17, 20, 22, 25, 26, 46, 48, 55–7, 59, 62, 135
M2, 6, 14, 25, 26, 29, 48, 58, 59
M3, 6, 7, 16, 17, 22, 23, 25, 26, 29, 31, 33, 34, 39, 48, 57, 58
£M3, 25, 26, 29, 33, 39, 46, 48, 50, 51, 54–9, 61, 62, 66–8, 71, 73, 74, 78, 80, 84, 86, 88, 127, 130, 140, 141
nominal, 12, 14–17, 32
own interest on (*see* Interest rate, on money)
purchasing power of, 13, 37
quantity of, 6, 12, 36, 43, 49, 50, 74
real, 13, 15, 26
(*see also* Demand for money)
Mortgages, 91, 133

National Institute of Economic and Social Research, The, 49, 51, 61
Non-bank,
customs, 101
financing, 114
institutions, 3, 114, 117, 137
intermediation, 93, 111, 114, 127
Non-clearing banks, 2, 6, 26, 88, 90, 93
Non-discriminatory,
policy, 8
system of control, 2, 9
North Sea oil, 54

Open market operations, 1, 36, 40, 62, 63, 65, 76, 108–10, 129

Parallel markets, 23, 139
Payments habits, 12, 20, 29
Pension funds, 3, 115
Phillips curve, 43, 59
Portfolio, 50, 63, 82, 93, 104, 110, 119
balance, 75
choice, 34
controls, 2
of currencies, 141
reallocation, 16, 32, 36, 50
Prudential requirements, 9, 71
controls, 63, 109
regulations, 102–17
Public sector borrowing requirement (PSBR), 58, 61, 68, 72, 74, 75, 84, 132, 133

Public sector debt, 52, 58, 61, 68, 71, 74, 75, 77, 79, 93

Radcliffe Committee, 14, 23, 65
Reduced form approach, 45
Retail,
banking, 90, 94, 100, 104, 113, 118–20, 128, 130, 137
business, 100, 114, 118, 120
deposits, 33, 100, 102
intermediacy, 93
market, 91, 101, 103
operations, 105

Savings,
accounts, 20
banks, 3, 51, 56, 59, 93, 115, 118, 135
deposits, 51, 56
personal, 43
Securities, 106, 122, 141
foreign, 13, 16, 51
government, 62, 77, 85
indexed-linked, 77, 78
long term, 13
public sector, 77
short term, 13, 76, 77, 88, 91
sterling, 72
Shares, 91
Special Deposits Scheme, 2, 3
Stock markets, 49
Supplementary Special Deposits, 1, 8, 31, 35, 72, 73, 81, 83, 84, 108, 109, 112–15, 120, 121, 123, 130, 138
Supply of money,
demand determined, 14, 31, 34, 46
nominal, 31
world, 141

Transmission mechanism, 45, 48–51
Trustee banks, 104

Velocity, 13, 27, 29, 31, 32, 146

Wages, 42, 43, 48, 51, 53, 81, 133
Wealth, 12, 13, 49, 51, 75
Wholesale,
banking, 86, 90, 94–102, 103, 104, 113, 118, 119, 127–30, 135, 137

Yields,
on bonds, 22
on consols, 13
on Treasury Bills, 9, 80